Building Probabilistic Graphical Models with Python

Solve machine learning problems using probabilistic graphical models implemented in Python with real-world applications

Kiran R Karkera

BIRMINGHAM - MUMBAI

Building Probabilistic Graphical Models with Python

Copyright © 2014 Packt Publishing

All rights reserved. No part of this book may be reproduced, stored in a retrieval system, or transmitted in any form or by any means, without the prior written permission of the publisher, except in the case of brief quotations embedded in critical articles or reviews.

Every effort has been made in the preparation of this book to ensure the accuracy of the information presented. However, the information contained in this book is sold without warranty, either express or implied. Neither the author, nor Packt Publishing, and its dealers and distributors will be held liable for any damages caused or alleged to be caused directly or indirectly by this book.

Packt Publishing has endeavored to provide trademark information about all of the companies and products mentioned in this book by the appropriate use of capitals. However, Packt Publishing cannot guarantee the accuracy of this information.

First published: June 2014

Production reference: 1190614

Published by Packt Publishing Ltd.
Livery Place
35 Livery Street
Birmingham B3 2PB, UK.

ISBN 978-1-78328-900-4

www.packtpub.com

Cover image by Manju Mohanadas (manju.mohanadas@gmail.com)

Credits

Author
Kiran R Karkera

Reviewers
Mohit Goenka
Shangpu Jiang
Jing (Dave) Tian
Xiao Xiao

Commissioning Editor
Kartikey Pandey

Acquisition Editor
Nikhil Chinnari

Content Development Editor
Madhuja Chaudhari

Technical Editor
Krishnaveni Haridas

Copy Editors
Alisha Aranha
Roshni Banerjee
Mradula Hegde

Project Coordinator
Melita Lobo

Proofreaders
Maria Gould
Joanna McMahon

Indexers
Mariammal Chettiyar
Hemangini Bari

Graphics
Disha Haria
Yuvraj Mannari
Abhinash Sahu

Production Coordinator
Alwin Roy

Cover Work
Alwin Roy

About the Author

Kiran R Karkera is a telecom engineer with a keen interest in machine learning. He has been programming professionally in Python, Java, and Clojure for more than 10 years. In his free time, he can be found attempting machine learning competitions at Kaggle and playing the flute.

> I would like to thank the maintainers of Libpgm and OpenGM libraries, Charles Cabot and Thorsten Beier, for their help with the code reviews.

About the Reviewers

Mohit Goenka graduated from the University of Southern California (USC) with a Master's degree in Computer Science. His thesis focused on game theory and human behavior concepts as applied in real-world security games. He also received an award for academic excellence from the Office of International Services at the University of Southern California. He has showcased his presence in various realms of computers including artificial intelligence, machine learning, path planning, multiagent systems, neural networks, computer vision, computer networks, and operating systems.

During his tenure as a student, Mohit won multiple competitions cracking codes and presented his work on *Detection of Untouched UFOs* to a wide range of audience. Not only is he a software developer by profession, but coding is also his hobby. He spends most of his free time learning about new technology and grooming his skills.

What adds a feather to Mohit's cap is his poetic skills. Some of his works are part of the University of Southern California libraries archived under the cover of the Lewis Carroll Collection. In addition to this, he has made significant contributions by volunteering to serve the community.

Shangpu Jiang is doing his PhD in Computer Science at the University of Oregon. He is interested in machine learning and data mining and has been working in this area for more than six years. He received his Bachelor's and Master's degrees from China.

Jing (Dave) Tian is now a graduate researcher and is doing his PhD in Computer Science at the University of Oregon. He is a member of the OSIRIS lab. His research direction involves system security, embedded system security, trusted computing, and static analysis for security and virtualization. He is interested in Linux kernel hacking and compilers. He also spent a year on AI and machine learning direction and taught the classes *Intro to Problem Solving using Python* and *Operating Systems* in the Computer Science department. Before that, he worked as a software developer in the Linux Control Platform (LCP) group at the Alcatel-Lucent (former Lucent Technologies) R&D department for around four years. He got his Bachelor's and Master's degrees from EE in China.

> Thanks to the author of this book who has done a good job for both Python and PGM; thanks to the editors of this book, who have made this book perfect and given me the opportunity to review such a nice book.

Xiao Xiao is a PhD student studying Computer Science at the University of Oregon. Her research interests lie in machine learning, especially probabilistic graphical models. Her previous project was to compare two inference algorithms' performance on a graphical model (relational dependency network).

www.PacktPub.com

Support files, eBooks, discount offers and more

You might want to visit `www.PacktPub.com` for support files and downloads related to your book.

Did you know that Packt offers eBook versions of every book published, with PDF and ePub files available? You can upgrade to the eBook version at `www.PacktPub.com` and as a print book customer, you are entitled to a discount on the eBook copy. Get in touch with us at `service@packtpub.com` for more details.

At `www.PacktPub.com`, you can also read a collection of free technical articles, sign up for a range of free newsletters and receive exclusive discounts and offers on Packt books and eBooks.

`http://PacktLib.PacktPub.com`

Do you need instant solutions to your IT questions? PacktLib is Packt's online digital book library. Here, you can access, read and search across Packt's entire library of books.

Why Subscribe?

- Fully searchable across every book published by Packt
- Copy and paste, print and bookmark content
- On demand and accessible via web browser

Free Access for Packt account holders

If you have an account with Packt at `www.PacktPub.com`, you can use this to access PacktLib today and view nine entirely free books. Simply use your login credentials for immediate access.

Table of Contents

Preface — 1

Chapter 1: Probability — 5
- The theory of probability — 5
- Goals of probabilistic inference — 8
- Conditional probability — 9
- The chain rule — 9
- The Bayes rule — 9
- Interpretations of probability — 11
- Random variables — 13
- Marginal distribution — 13
- Joint distribution — 14
- Independence — 14
- Conditional independence — 15
- Types of queries — 16
  - Probability queries — 16
  - MAP queries — 16
- Summary — 18

Chapter 2: Directed Graphical Models — 19
- Graph terminology — 19
  - Python digression — 20
- Independence and independent parameters — 20
- The Bayes network — 23
  - The chain rule — 24
- Reasoning patterns — 24
  - Causal reasoning — 25
  - Evidential reasoning — 27
  - Inter-causal reasoning — 27

D-separation	29
The D-separation example	31
Blocking and unblocking a V-structure	33
Factorization and I-maps	34
The Naive Bayes model	34
The Naive Bayes example	36
Summary	37

Chapter 3: Undirected Graphical Models — 39

Pairwise Markov networks	39
The Gibbs distribution	41
An induced Markov network	43
Factorization	43
Flow of influence	44
Active trail and separation	45
Structured prediction	45
Problem of correlated features	46
The CRF representation	46
The CRF example	47
The factorization-independence tango	48
Summary	49

Chapter 4: Structure Learning — 51

The structure learning landscape	52
Constraint-based structure learning	52
Part I	52
Part II	53
Part III	54
Summary of constraint-based approaches	60
Score-based learning	60
The likelihood score	61
The Bayesian information criterion score	62
The Bayesian score	63
Summary of score-based learning	68
Summary	68

Chapter 5: Parameter Learning — 69

The likelihood function	71
Parameter learning example using MLE	72
MLE for Bayesian networks	74
Bayesian parameter learning example using MLE	75
Data fragmentation	77

Effects of data fragmentation on parameter estimation	77
Bayesian parameter estimation	79
An example of Bayesian methods for parameter learning	80
Bayesian estimation for the Bayesian network	85
Example of Bayesian estimation	85
Summary	91

Chapter 6: Exact Inference Using Graphical Models — 93

Complexity of inference	93
Real-world issues	94
Using the Variable Elimination algorithm	94
Marginalizing factors that are not relevant	97
Factor reduction to filter evidence	98
Shortcomings of the brute-force approach	100
Using the Variable Elimination approach	100
Complexity of Variable Elimination	106
Graph perspective	107
Learning the induced width from the graph structure	109
The tree algorithm	110
The four stages of the junction tree algorithm	111
Using the junction tree algorithm for inference	112
Stage 1.1 – moralization	113
Stage 1.2 – triangulation	114
Stage 1.3 – building the join tree	114
Stage 2 – initializing potentials	115
Stage 3 – message passing	115
Summary	119

Chapter 7: Approximate Inference Methods — 121

The optimization perspective	121
Belief propagation in general graphs	122
Creating a cluster graph to run LBP	123
Message passing in LBP	124
Steps in the LBP algorithm	125
Improving the convergence of LBP	126
Applying LBP to segment an image	126
Understanding energy-based models	128
Visualizing unary and pairwise factors on a 3 x 3 grid	129
Creating a model for image segmentation	130
Applications of LBP	135
Sampling-based methods	136
Forward sampling	136
The accept-reject sampling method	137

The Markov Chain Monte Carlo sampling process	138
The Markov property	138
The Markov chain	139
Reaching a steady state	140
Sampling using a Markov chain	140
Gibbs sampling	141
Steps in the Gibbs sampling procedure	141
An example of Gibbs sampling	142
Summary	**145**
Appendix: References	**147**
Index	**151**

Preface

In this book, we start with an exploratory tour of the basics of graphical models, their types, why they are used, and what kind of problems they solve. We then explore subproblems in the context of graphical models, such as their representation, building them, learning their structure and parameters, and using them to answer our inference queries.

This book attempts to give just enough information on the theory, and then use code samples to peep under the hood to understand how some of the algorithms are implemented. The code sample also provides a handy template to build graphical models and answer our probability queries. Of the many kinds of graphical models described in the literature, this book primarily focuses on discrete Bayesian networks, with occasional examples from Markov networks.

What this book covers

Chapter 1, *Probability*, covers the concepts of probability required to understand the graphical models.

Chapter 2, *Directed Graphical Models*, provides information about Bayesian networks, their properties related to independence, conditional independence, and D-separation. This chapter uses code snippets to load a Bayes network and understand its independence properties.

Chapter 3, *Undirected Graphical Models*, covers the properties of Markov networks, how they are different from Bayesian networks, and their independence properties.

Chapter 4, *Structure Learning*, covers multiple approaches to infer the structure of the Bayesian network using a dataset. We also learn the computational complexity of structure learning and use code snippets in this chapter to learn the structures given in the sampled datasets.

Chapter 5, *Parameter Learning*, covers the maximum likelihood and Bayesian approaches to parameter learning with code samples from PyMC.

Chapter 6, *Exact Inference Using Graphical Models*, explains the Variable Elimination algorithm for accurate inference and explores code snippets that answer our inference queries using the same algorithm.

Chapter 7, *Approximate Inference Methods*, explores the approximate inference for networks that are too large to run exact inferences on. We will also go through the code samples that run approximate inferences using loopy belief propagation on Markov networks.

Appendix, *References*, includes all the links and URLs that will help to easily understand the chapters in the book.

What you need for this book

To run the code samples in the book, you'll need a laptop or desktop with IPython installed. We use several software packages in this book, most of them can be installed using the Python installation procedure such as `pip` or `easy_install`. In some cases, the software needs to be compiled from the source and may require a C++ compiler.

Who this book is for

This book is aimed at developers conversant with Python and who wish to explore the nuances of graphical models using code samples.

This book is also ideal for students who have been theoretically introduced to graphical models and wish to realize the implementations of graphical models and get a feel for the capabilities of different (graphical model) libraries to deal with real-world models.

Machine-learning practitioners familiar with classification and regression models and who wish to explore and experiment with the types of problems graphical models can solve will also find this book an invaluable resource.

This book looks at graphical models as a tool that can be used to solve problems in the machine-learning domain. Moreover, it does not attempt to explain the mathematical underpinnings of graphical models or go into details of the steps for each algorithm used.

Conventions

In this book, you will find a number of styles of text that distinguish between different kinds of information. Here are some examples of these styles, and an explanation of their meaning.

Code words in text, database table names, folder names, filenames, file extensions, pathnames, dummy URLs, user input, and Twitter handles are shown as follows: "We can do the same by creating a `TfidfVectorizer` object."

A block of code is set as follows:

```
clf = MultinomialNB(alpha=.01)
print "CrossValidation Score: ", np.mean(cross_validation.cross_val_score(clf,vectors, newsgroups.target, scoring='f1'))
CrossValidation Score:   0.954618416381
```

> Warnings or important notes appear in a box like this.

> Tips and tricks appear like this.

Reader feedback

Feedback from our readers is always welcome. Let us know what you think about this book—what you liked or may have disliked. Reader feedback is important for us to develop titles that you really get the most out of.

To send us general feedback, simply send an e-mail to feedback@packtpub.com, and mention the book title via the subject of your message.

If there is a topic that you have expertise in and you are interested in either writing or contributing to a book, see our author guide on www.packtpub.com/authors.

Customer support

Now that you are the proud owner of a Packt book, we have a number of things to help you to get the most from your purchase.

Downloading the example code

You can download the example code files for all Packt books you have purchased from your account at `http://www.packtpub.com`. If you purchased this book elsewhere, you can visit `http://www.packtpub.com/support` and register to have the files e-mailed directly to you.

Errata

Although we have taken every care to ensure the accuracy of our content, mistakes do happen. If you find a mistake in one of our books—maybe a mistake in the text or the code—we would be grateful if you would report this to us. By doing so, you can save other readers from frustration and help us improve subsequent versions of this book. If you find any errata, please report them by visiting `http://www.packtpub.com/submit-errata`, selecting your book, clicking on the **errata submission form** link, and entering the details of your errata. Once your errata are verified, your submission will be accepted and the errata will be uploaded on our website, or added to any list of existing errata, under the Errata section of that title. Any existing errata can be viewed by selecting your title from `http://www.packtpub.com/support`.

Piracy

Piracy of copyright material on the Internet is an ongoing problem across all media. At Packt, we take the protection of our copyright and licenses very seriously. If you come across any illegal copies of our works, in any form, on the Internet, please provide us with the location address or website name immediately so that we can pursue a remedy.

Please contact us at `copyright@packtpub.com` with a link to the suspected pirated material.

We appreciate your help in protecting our authors, and our ability to bring you valuable content.

Questions

You can contact us at `questions@packtpub.com` if you are having a problem with any aspect of the book, and we will do our best to address it.

1
Probability

Before we embark on the journey through the land of graphical models, we must equip ourselves with some tools that will aid our understanding. We will first start with a tour of probability and its concepts such as random variables and the types of distributions.

We will then try to understand the types of questions that probability can help us answer and the multiple interpretations of probability. Finally, we will take a quick look at the Bayes rule, which helps us understand the relationships between probabilities, and also look at the accompanying concepts of conditional probabilities and the chain rule.

The theory of probability

We often encounter situations where we have to exercise our subjective belief about an event's occurrence; for example, events such as weather or traffic that are inherently stochastic. Probability can also be understood as the degree of subjective belief.

When we talk about the weather (for example, this evening), it is understood that the weather can have multiple outcomes such as rainy, sunny, or cloudy. The space of all the possible outcomes is said to be an event (also called the sample space). For example, the outcomes of a throw of a dice would be a set of numbers from 1 to 6. While dealing with measurable outcomes such as the throw of a dice or today's weather (which can be rainy, sunny, or cloudy), we can assign a probability value to each outcome to encapsulate our degree of belief in those outcomes. An example of the notation used to express our belief is *P(rainy)=0.3*, which can be read as the probability of rain is 0.3 or 30 percent.

Probability

The axioms of probability that have been formulated by Kolmogorov are stated as follows:

- The probability of an event is a non-negative real number (that is, the probability that it will rain today may be small, but nevertheless will be greater than or equal to 0). This is explained in mathematical terms as follows:

$$P(E) \in \mathbb{R}, P(E) \geq 0 \quad \forall E \in F \text{ where } F \text{ is the event space}$$

- The probability of the occurrence of some event in the sample space is 1 (that is, if the weather events in our sample space are rainy, sunny, and cloudy, then one of these events has to occur), as shown in the following formula:

$$P(\Omega) = 1 \text{ where } \Omega \text{ is the sample space}$$

- The sum of the probabilities of mutually exclusive events gives their union, as given in the following formula:

$$P(E_1 \cup E_2 \cup \ldots) = \sum_{i=1}^{\infty} P(E_i)$$

When we discuss about the fairness (or unfairness) of a dice or a coin flip, we are discussing another key aspect of probability, that is, model parameters. The idea of a fair coin translates to the fact that the controlling parameter has a value of 0.5 in favor of heads, which also translates to the fact that we assume all the outcomes to be equally likely. Later in the book, we shall examine how many parameters are required to completely specify a probability distribution. However, we are getting ahead of ourselves. First let's learn about probability distribution.

A probability distribution consists of the probabilities associated with each measurable outcome. In the case of a discrete outcome (such as a throw of a dice or a coin flip), the distribution is specified by a probability mass function, and in the case of a continuous outcome (such as the height of students in a class), it is specified by a probability density function.

Let us see discrete distributions with an example. A coin flip has two outcomes: heads and tails, and a fair coin assigns equal probabilities to all outcomes. This means that the probability distribution is simple—for heads, it is 0.5 and for tails, it is 0.5. A distribution like this (for example, heads 0.3 and tails 0.7) would be the one that corresponds to a biased coin. The following graph shows the discrete probability distribution for the sum of values when two dice are thrown:

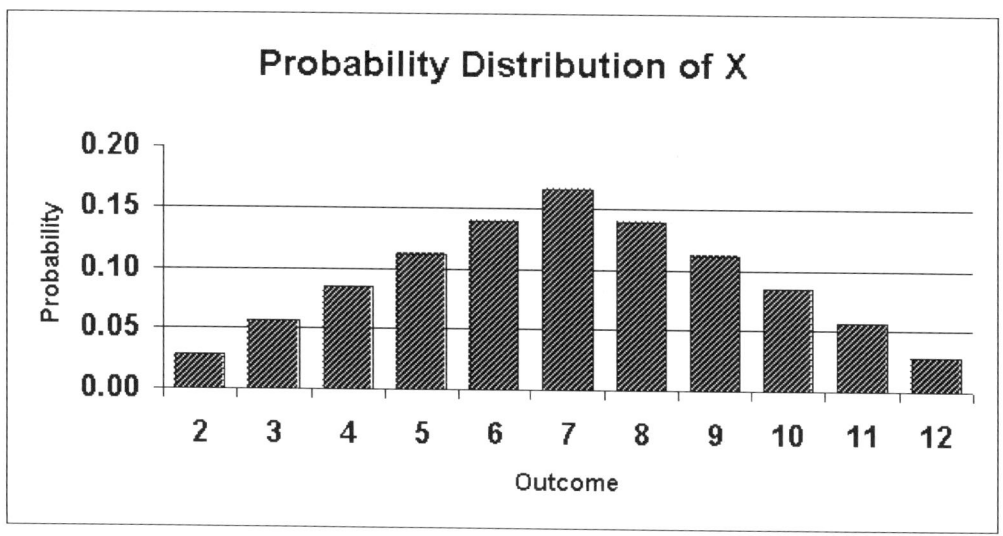

A distribution that assigns equal probabilities to all outcomes is called a uniform distribution. This is one of the many distributions that we will explore.

Let's look at one of the common distributions associated with continuous outcomes, that is, the Gaussian or normal distribution, which is in the shape of a bell and hence called a bell curve (though there are other distributions whose shapes are similar to the bell shape). The following are some examples from the real world:

- Heights of students in a class are log-normally distributed (if we take the logarithm of the heights of students and plot it, the resulting distribution is normally distributed)
- Measurement errors in physical experiments

A Gaussian distribution has two parameters: mean (μ) and variance (σ^2). The parameters mean and variance determine the middle point and the dispersion of the distribution away from the mean, respectively.

Probability

The following graph shows multiple Gaussian distributions with different values of mean and variance. It can be seen that the more variance there is, the broader the distribution, whereas the value of the mean shifts the peak on the *x* axis, as shown in the following graph:

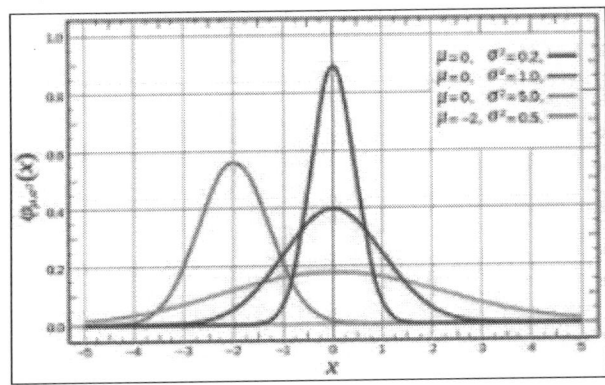

Goals of probabilistic inference

Now that we have understood the concept of probability, we must ask ourselves how this is used. The kind of questions that we ask fall into the following categories:

- The first question is parameter estimation, such as, is a coin biased or fair? And if biased, what is the value of the parameter?
- The second question is that given the parameters, what is the probability of the data? For example, what is the probability of five heads in a row if we flip a coin where the bias (or parameter) is known.

  The preceding questions depend on the data (or lack of it). If we have a set of observations of a coin flip, we can estimate the controlling parameter (that is, parameter estimation). If we have an estimate of the parameter, we would like to estimate the probability of the data generated by the coin flips (the second question). Then, there are times when we go back and forth to improve the model.

- Is the model well-suited to the problem, is the third question that we may enquire about. Is there a single parameter that controls the results of the coin flipping experiment? When we wish to model a complicated phenomena (such as the traffic or weather prediction), there certainly exist several parameters in the model, where hundreds or even thousands of parameters are not unusual. In such cases, the question that we're trying to ask is, which model fits the data better? We shall see some examples in the later chapters on different aspects of model fit.

Conditional probability

Let us use a concrete example, where we have a population of candidates who are applying for a job. One event (x) could be a set of all candidates who get an offer, whereas another event (y) could be the set of all highly experienced candidates. We might want to reason about the set of a conjoint event ($x \cap y$), which is the set of experienced candidates who got an offer (the probability of a conjoint event $P(x \cap y)$ is also written as $P(x, y)$). The question that raises is that if we know that one event has occurred, does it change the probability of occurrence of the other event. In this case, if we know for sure that a candidate got an offer, what does it tell us about their experience?

Conditional probability is formally defined as $P(x|y) = \frac{P(x \cap y)}{P(y)}$, which can be read as the probability of x given that y occurred. The denominator $P(y)$ is the sum of all possible outcomes of the joint distribution with the value of x summed out, that is, $\sum_x P(x, y) = P(y)$.

The chain rule

The chain rule allows us to calculate the joint distribution of a set of random variables using their conditional probabilities. In other words, the joint distribution is the product of individual conditional probabilities. Since $P(x \cap y) = P(x)P(y|x)$, and if $a_1, a_2 \ldots a_n$ are events, $P(a_1 \cap \ldots \cap a_n) = P(a_1)P(a_2|a_1)\ldots P(a_{n-1}|a_n)$.

We shall return to this in detail in graphical models, where the chain rule helps us decompose a big problem (computing the joint distribution) by splitting it into smaller problems (conditional probabilities).

The Bayes rule

The Bayes rule is one of the foundations of the probability theory, and we won't go into much detail here. It follows from the definition of conditional probability, as shown in the following formula:

$$P(x|y) = \frac{P(y|x)P(x)}{P(y)}$$

From the formula, we can infer the following about the Bayes rule—we entertain prior beliefs about the problem we are reasoning about. This is simply called the prior term. When we start to see the data, our beliefs change, which gives rise to our final belief (called the posterior), as shown in the following formula:

$$posterior \; \alpha \; prior \times likelihood$$

Let us see the intuition behind the Bayes rule with an example. Amy and Carl are standing at a railway station waiting for a train. Amy has been catching the same train everyday for the past year, and it is Carl's first day at the station. What would be their prior beliefs about the train being on time?

Amy has been catching the train daily for the past year, and she has always seen the train arrive within two minutes of the scheduled departure time. Therefore, her strong belief is that the train will be at most two minutes late. Since it is Carl's first day, he has no idea about the train's punctuality. However, Carl has been traveling the world in the past year, and has been in places where trains are not known to be punctual. Therefore, he has a weak belief that the train could be even 30 minutes late.

On day one, the train arrives 5 minutes late. The effect this observation has on both Amy and Carl is different. Since Amy has a strong prior, her beliefs are modified a little bit to accept that the train can be as late as 5 minutes. Carl's beliefs now change in the direction that the trains here are rather punctual.

In other words, the posterior beliefs are influenced in multiple ways: when someone with a strong prior sees a few observations, their posterior belief does not change much as compared to their prior. On the other hand, when someone with a weak prior sees numerous observations (a strong likelihood), their posterior belief changes a lot and is influenced largely by the observations (likelihood) rather than their prior belief.

Let's look at a numerical example of the Bayes rule. D is the event that an athlete uses **performance-enhancing drugs** (**PEDs**). T is the event that the drug test returns positive. Throughout the discussion, we use the prime (') symbol to notate that the event didn't occur; for example, D' represents the event that the athlete didn't use PEDs.

$P(D|T)$ is the probability that the athlete used PEDs given that the drug test returned positive. $P(T|D)$ is the probability that the drug test returned positive given that the athlete used PEDs.

The lab doing the drug test claims that it can detect PEDs 90 percent of the time. We also learn that the false-positive rate (athletes whose tests are positive but did not use PEDs) is 15 percent, and that 10 percent of athletes use PEDs. What is the probability that an athlete uses PEDs if the drug test returned positive?

From the basic form of the Bayes rule, we can write the following formula:

$$P(D|T) = \frac{P(T|D)P(D)}{P(T|D)P(D) + P(T|D')P(D')}$$

Now, we have the following data:

- $P(T|D)$: This is equal to 0.90
- $P(T|D')$: This is equal to 0.15 (the test that returns positive given that the athlete didn't use PEDs)
- $P(D)$: This is equal to 0.1

    When we substitute these values, we get the final value as 0.4, as shown in the following formula:

$$P(D|T) = \frac{0.9 \times 0.1}{0.9 \times 0.1 + 0.15 \times 0.9} = 0.4$$

This result seems a little counterintuitive in the sense that despite testing positive for PEDs, there's only a 40 percent chance that the athlete used PEDs. This is because the use of PEDs itself is quite low (only 10 percent of athletes use PEDs), and that the rate of false positives is relatively high (0.15 percent).

Interpretations of probability

In the previous example, we noted how we have a prior belief and that the introduction of the observed data can change our beliefs. That viewpoint, however, is one of the multiple interpretations of probability.

The first one (which we have discussed already) is a Bayesian interpretation, which holds that probability is a degree of belief, and that the degree of belief changes before and after accounting for evidence.

The second view is called the Frequentist interpretation, where probability measures the proportion of outcomes and posits that the prior belief is an incorrect notion that is not backed up by data.

To illustrate this with an example, let's go back to the coin flipping experiment, where we wish to learn the bias of the coin. We run two experiments, where we flip the coin 10 times and 10000 times, respectively. In the first experiment, we get 7 heads and in the second experiment, we get 7000 heads.

From a Frequentist viewpoint, in both the experiments, the probability of getting heads is 0.7 (7/10 or 7000/10000). However, we can easily convince ourselves that we have a greater degree of belief in the outcome of the second experiment than that of the first experiment. This is because the first experiment's outcome has a Bayesian perspective that if we had a prior belief, the second experiment's observations would overwhelm the prior, which is unlikely in the first experiment.

For the discussion in the following sections, let us consider an example of a company that is interviewing candidates for a job. Prior to inviting the candidate for an interview, the candidate is screened based on the amount of experience that the candidate has as well as the GPA score that the candidate received in his graduation results. If the candidate passes the screening, he is called for an interview. Once the candidate has been interviewed, the company may make the candidate a job offer (which is based on the candidate's performance in the interview). The candidate is also evaluating going for a postgraduate degree, and the candidate's admission to a postgraduate degree course of his choice depends on his grades in the bachelor's degree. The following diagram is a visual representation of our understanding of the relationships between the factors that affect the job selection (and postgraduate degree admission) criteria:

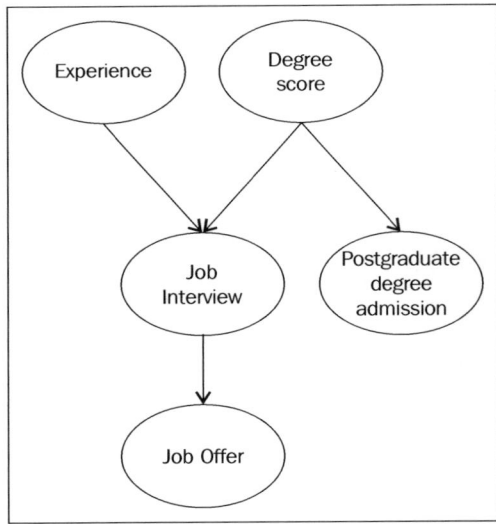

Random variables

The classical notion of a random variable is the one whose value is subject to variations due to chance (Wikipedia). Most programmers have encountered random numbers from standard libraries in programming languages. From a programmer's perspective, unlike normal variables, a random variable returns a new value every time its value is read, where the value of the variable could be the result of a new invocation of a random number generator.

We have seen the concept of events earlier, and how we could consider the probability of a single event occurring out of the set of measurable events. It may be suitable, however, to consider the attributes of an outcome.

In the candidate's job search example, one of the attributes of a candidate is his experience. This attribute can take multiple values such as highly relevant or not relevant. The formal machinery for discussing attributes and their values in different outcomes is called random variables [Koller et al, 2.1.3.1].

Random variables can take on categorical values (such as *{Heads, Tails}* for the outcomes of a coin flip) or real values (such as the heights of students in a class).

Marginal distribution

We have seen that the job hunt example (described in the previous diagram) has five random variables. They are *grades, experience, interview, offer,* and *admission*. These random variables have a corresponding set of events.

Now, let us consider a subset X of random variables, where X contains only the *Experience* random variable. This subset contains the events *highly relevant* and *not relevant*.

If we were to enlist the probabilities of all the events in the subset X, it would be called a marginal distribution, an example of which can be found in the following formula:

$$P(Experience = 'Highly\ relevant') = 0.4, P(Experience = 'Not\ Relevant') = 0.6$$

Like all valid distributions, the probabilities should sum up to 1.

The set of random variables (over which the marginal distribution is described) can contain just one variable (as in the previous example), or it could contain several variables, such as *{Experience, Grades, Interview}*.

Joint distribution

We have seen that the marginal distribution is a distribution that describes a subset of random variables. Next, we will discuss a distribution that describes all the random variables in the set. This is called a joint distribution. Let us look at the joint distribution that involves the *Degree score* and *Experience* random variables in the job hunt example:

		Relevant Experience		
		Highly relevant	Not relevant	
Degree score	Poor	0.1	0.1	0.2
	Average	0.1	0.4	0.5
	Excellent	0.2	0.1	0.3
		0.4	0.6	1

The values within the dark gray-colored cells are of the joint distribution, and the values in the light gray-colored cells are of the marginal distribution (sometimes called that because they are written on the margins). It can be observed that the individual marginal distributions sum up to 1, just like a normal probability distribution.

Once the joint distribution is described, the marginal distribution can be found by summing up individual rows or columns. In the preceding table, if we sum up the columns, the first column gives us the probability for *Highly relevant*, and the second column for *Not relevant*. It can be seen that a similar tactic applied on the rows gives us the probabilities for degree scores.

Independence

The concept of independent events can be understood by looking at an example. Suppose we have two dice, and when we roll them together, we get a score of 2 on one die and a score of 3 on the other. It is not difficult to see that the two events are independent of each other because the outcome of a roll of each dice does not influence or interact with the other one.

We can define the concept of independence in multiple ways. Assume that we have two events a and b and the probability of the conjunction of both events is simply the product of their probabilities, as shown in the following formula:

$$P(a,b) = P(a)P(b)$$

If we were to write the probability of $P(a,b)$ as $P(a)P(b|a)$ (that is, the product of probability of *a* and probability of *b* given that the event *a* has happened), if the events *a* and *b* are independent, they resolve to $P(a)P(b)$.

An alternate way of specifying independence is by saying that the probability of *a* given *b* is simply the probability of *a*, that is, the occurrence of *b* does not affect the probability of *a*, as shown in the following formula:

$$P = (a \perp b) \text{ if } P(a|b) = P(a) \text{ or if } P(b) = 0$$

It can be seen that the independence is symmetric, that is, $(a \perp b)$ *implies* $(b \perp a)$. Although this definition of independence is in the context of events, the same concept can be generalized to the independence of random variables.

Conditional independence

Given two events, it is not always obvious to determine whether they are independent or not. Consider a job applicant who applied for a job at two companies, Facebook and Google. It could result in two events, the first being that a candidate gets an interview call from Google, and another event that he gets an interview call from Facebook. Does knowing the outcome of the first event tell us anything about the probability of the second event? Yes, it does, because we can reason that if a candidate is smart enough to get a call from Google, he is a promising candidate, and that the probability of a call from Facebook is quite high.

What has been established so far is that both events are not independent. Supposing we learn that the companies decide to send an interview invite based on the candidate's grades, and we learn that the candidate has an A grade, from which we infer that the candidate is fairly intelligent. We can reason that since the candidate is fairly smart, knowing that the candidate got an interview call from Google does not tell us anything more about his perceived intelligence, and that it doesn't change the probability of the interview call from Facebook. This can be formally annotated as the probability of a Facebook interview call, given a Google interview call AND grade A, is equal to the probability of a Facebook interview call given grade A, as shown in the following formula:

$$Pr(Facebook | Google, GradeA) = Pr(Facebook | GradeA)$$

In other words, we are saying that the invite from Facebook is conditionally independent of the invite from Google, given the candidate has grade A.

Types of queries

Having learned about joint and conditional probability distributions, let us turn our attention to the types of queries we can pose to these distributions.

Probability queries

This is the most common type of query, and it consists of the following two parts:

- **The evidence**: This is a subset E of random variables which have been observed
- **The query**: This is a subset Y of random variables

We wish to compute the value of the probability $P(Y | E = e)$, which is the posterior probability or the marginal probability over Y. Using the job seeker example again, we can compute the marginal distribution over an interview call, conditioned on the fact that *Degree score = Grade A*.

MAP queries

Maximum a posteriori (MAP) is the highest probability joint assignment to some subsets of variables. In the case of the probability query, it is the value of the probability that matters. In the case of MAP, calculating the exact probability value of the joint assignment is secondary as compared to the task of finding the joint assignment to all the random variables.

It is possible to return multiple joint assignments if the probability values are equal. We shall see from an example that in the case of the joint assignment, it is possible that the highest probability from each marginal value may not be the highest joint assignment (the following example is from Koller et al).

Consider two non-independent random variables X and Y, where Y is dependent on X. The following table shows the probability distribution over X:

X0	X1
0.4	0.6

We can see that the MAP assignment for the random variable X is *X1* since it has a higher value. The following table shows the marginal distribution over X and Y:

P(Y|X)	Y0	Y1
X0	0.1	0.9
X1	0.5	0.5

The joint distribution over X and Y is listed in the following table:

Assignment	Value
X0, Y0	0.04
X0, Y1	0.36
X1, Y0	0.3
X1, Y1	0.3

In the joint distribution shown in the preceding table, the MAP assignment to random variables (X, Y) is (X0, Y1), and that the MAP assignment to X (X1) is not a part of the MAP of the joint assignment. To sum up, the MAP assignment cannot be obtained by simply taking the maximum probability value in the marginal distribution for each random variable.

A different type of MAP query is a marginal MAP query where we only have a subset of the variables that forms the query, as opposed to the joint distribution. In the previous example, a marginal MAP query would be MAP (Y), which is the maximum value of the MAP assignment to the random variable Y, which can be read by looking at the joint distribution and summing out the values of X. From the following table, we can read the maximum value and determine that the MAP (Y) is Y1:

Assignment	Value
Y0	0.34
Y1	0.66

 The data for the marginal query has been obtained from *Querying Joint Probability Distributions* by Sargur Srihari. You can find it at http://www.cedar.buffalo.edu/~srihari/CSE574/Chap8/Ch8-PGM-Directed/8.1.2-QueryingProbabilityDistributions.pdf.

Summary

In this chapter, we looked at the concepts of basic probability, random variables, and the Bayes theorem. We also learned about the chain rule and joint and marginal distributions with the use of a candidate job search example, which we shall return to in the later chapters. Having obtained a good grasp on these topics, we can now move on to exploring Bayes and Markov networks in the forthcoming chapters, where we will formally describe these networks to answer some of the probability queries we discussed in this chapter. While this chapter was completely theoretical, from the next chapter, we shall implement the Python code to seek answers to our questions.

2
Directed Graphical Models

In this chapter, we shall learn about directed graphical models, which are also known as Bayesian networks. We start with the what (the problem we are trying to solve), the how (graph representation), the why (factorization and the equivalence of CPD and graph factorization), and then move on to using the Libpgm Python library to play with a small Bayes net.

Graph terminology

Before we jump into Bayes nets, let's learn some graph terminology. A graph G consists of a set of nodes (also called vertices) $V = \{V_1, V_2, \ldots V_n\}$ and another set of edges $E = \{E_1, E_2, \ldots E_n\}$. An edge that connects a pair of nodes V_i, V_j can be of two types: directed (represented by $V_i \rightarrow V_j$) and undirected (represented by $V_i - V_j$). A graph can also be represented as an adjacency matrix, which in the case of an undirected graph, if the position $G(i,j)$ contains 1, indicates an edge between i and j vertices. In the case of a directed graph, a value of 1 or -1 indicates the direction of the edge.

In many cases, we are interested in graphs in which all the edges are either directed or undirected, leading to them being called directed graphs or undirected graphs, respectively.

The parents of a V_1 node in a directed graph are the set of nodes that have outgoing edges that terminate at V_1.

The children of the V_1 node are the set of nodes that have incoming edges which leave V_1.

The degree of a node is the number of edges it participates in.

A clique is a set of nodes where every pair of nodes is connected by an edge. A maximal clique is the one that loses the clique property if it includes any other node.

If there exists a path from a node that returns to itself after traversing the other nodes, it is called a cycle or loop.

A **Directed Acyclic Graph** (**DAG**) is a graph with no cycles.

A **Partially Directed Acyclic Graph** (**PDAG**) is a graph that can contain both directed and undirected edges.

A forest is a set of trees.

Python digression

We will soon start to explore GMs using Python, and this is a good time to review your Python installation. The recommended base Python installation for the examples in this book is IPython, which is available for all platforms. Refer to the IPython website for platform-specific documentation.

We shall also use multiple Python libraries to explore various areas of graphical models. Unless otherwise specified, the usual way to install Python libraries is using `pip install <packagename>` or `easy_install <packagename>`.

To use the code in this chapter, please install Libpgm (`https://pypi.python.org/pypi/libpgm`) and scipy (`http://scipy.org/`).

Independence and independent parameters

One of the key problems that graphical models solve is in defining the joint distribution. Let's take a look at the job interview example where a candidate with a certain amount of experience and education is looking for a job. The candidate is also applying for admission to a higher education program.

We are trying to fully specify the joint distribution over the job offer, which (according to our intuition) depends on the outcome of the job interview, the candidate's experience, and his grades (we assume that the candidate's admission into a graduate school is not considered relevant for the job offer). Three random variables *{Offer, Experience, Grades}* take two values (such as yes and no for the job offer and highly relevant and not relevant for the job experience) and the interview takes on three values, and the joint distribution will be represented by a table that has 24 rows (that is, 2 x 2 x 2 x 3).

Each row contains a probability for the assignment of the random variables in that row. While different instantiations of the table might have different probability assignments, we will need 24 parameters (one for each row) to encode the information in the table. However, for calculation purposes, we will need only 23 independent parameters. Why do we remove one? Since the sum of probabilities equals 1, the last parameter can be calculated by subtracting one from the sum of the 23 parameters already found.

	Experience	Grades	Interview	Offer	Probability
0	0	0	0	0	0.7200
1	0	0	0	1	0.0800
2	0	0	1	0	0.0720
3	0	0	1	1	0.1080
.					
.					
Rows elided					
21	1	1	1	1	0.1200
22	1	1	2	0	0.0070
23	1	1	2	1	0.6930

The preceding joint distribution is the output of the `printjointdistribution.ipynb` IPython Notebook, which prints all permutations of the random variables' experience, grades, interview, and offer, along with their probabilities.

It should be clear on observing the preceding table that acquiring a fully specified joint distribution is difficult due to the following reasons:

- It is too big to store and manipulate from a computational point of view
- We'll need large amounts of data for each assignment of the joint distribution to correctly elicit the probabilities
- The individual probabilities in a large joint distribution become vanishingly small and are no longer meaningful to human comprehension

How can we avoid having to specify the joint distribution? We can do this by using the concept of independent parameters, which we shall explore in the following example.

Directed Graphical Models

The joint distribution P over **Grades** and **Admission** is (throughout this book, the superscript 0 and 1 indicate low and high scores) as follows:

Grades	Admission	Probability (S,A)
S^0	A^0	0.665
S^0	A^1	0.035
S^1	A^0	0.06
S^1	A^1	0.24

When we reason about graduate admissions from the perspective of causality, it is clear that the admission depends on the grades, which can also be represented using the conditional probability as follows:

$$P(S,A) = P(S)P(A|S)$$

The number of parameters required in the preceding formula is three, one parameter for $P(S)$ and two each for $P(A|S^0)$ and $P(A|S^1)$. Since this is a simple distribution, the number of parameters required is the same for both conditional and joint distributions, but let's observe the complete network to see if the conditional parameterization makes a difference:

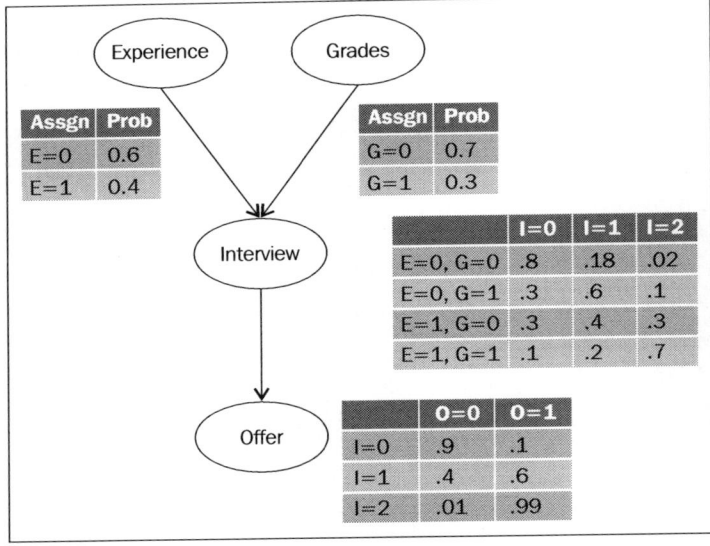

How do we calculate the number of parameters in the Bayes net in the preceding diagram? Let's go through each conditional probability table, one parameter at a time. **Experience** and **Grades** take two values, and therefore need one independent parameter each. The **Interview** table has 12 (3 x 4) parameters. However, each row sums up to 1, and therefore, we need two independent parameters per row. The whole table needs 8 (2 x 4) independent parameters. Similarly, the **Offer** table has six entries, but only 1 independent parameter per row is required, which makes 3 (1 x 3) independent parameters. Therefore, the total number of parameters is 1 (Experience) + 1 (Grades)+ 12 (Interview) + 3 (Offer) amount to 17, which is a lot lesser than 24 parameters to fully specify the joint distribution. Therefore, the independence assumptions in the Bayesian network helps us avoid specifying the joint distribution.

The Bayes network

A Bayes network is a structure that can be represented as a directed acyclic graph, and the data it contains can be seen from the following two points of view:

- It allows a compact and modular representation of the joint distribution using the chain rule for Bayes network
- It allows the conditional independence assumptions between vertices to be observed

We shall explore the two ideas in the job interview example that we have seen so far (which is a Bayesian network, by the way).

The modular structure of the Bayes network is the set of local probability models that represent the nature of the dependence of each variable on its parents (Koller et al 3.2.1.1). One probability distribution each exists for *Experience* and *Grades*, and a **conditional probability distribution** (**CPD**) each exists for *Interview* and *Offer*. A CPD specifies a distribution over a random variable, given all the combinations of assignments to its parents. Thus, the modular representation for a given Bayes network is the set of CPDs for each random variable.

The conditional independence viewpoint flows from the edges (our intuition draws) between different random variables, where we presume that a call for a job interview must be dependent on a candidate's experience as well as the score he received in his degree course, and the probability of a job offer depends solely on the outcome of the job interview.

The chain rule

The chain rule allows us to define the joint distribution as a product of factors. In the job interview example, using the chain rule for probability, we can write the following formula:

$$P(E,G,I,O) = P(E) \times P(G|E) \times P(I|E,G) \times P(O|E,G,I)$$

In the preceding formula, *E*, *G*, *I*, and *O* stand for *Experience*, *Grades*, *Interview*, and *Offer* respectively. However, we can use the conditional independence assumptions encoded by the graph to rewrite the joint distribution as follows:

$$P(E,G,I,O) = P(E) \times P(G) \times P(I|E,G) \times P(O|I)$$

This is an example of the chain rule for Bayesian networks. More generally, we can write it as follows:

$$P(X_1, X_2, \ldots, X_n) = \prod i\, P(X_i | Par_G(X_i))$$

Here, X_i is a node in the graph G and Par_G are the parents of the X_i node in the graph G.

Reasoning patterns

In this section, we shall look at different kinds of reasoning used in a Bayes network. We shall use the Libpgm library to create a Bayes network. Libpgm reads the network information such as nodes, edges, and CPD probabilities associated with each node from a JSON-formatted file with a specific format. This JSON file is read into the `NodeData` and `GraphSkeleton` objects to create a discrete Bayesian network (which, as the name suggests, is a Bayes network where the CPDs take discrete values). The `TableCPDFactorization` object is an object that wraps the discrete Bayesian network and allows us to query the CPDs in the network. The JSON file for this example, `job_interview.txt`, should be placed in the same folder as the IPython Notebook so that it can be loaded automatically.

The following discussion uses integers 0, 1, and 2 for discrete outcomes of each random variable, where 0 is the worst outcome. For example, *Interview* = 0 indicates the worst outcome of the interview and *Interview* = 2 is the best outcome.

Causal reasoning

The first kind of reasoning we shall explore is called causal reasoning. Initially, we observe the prior probability of an event unconditioned by any evidence (for this example, we shall focus on the *Offer* random variable). We then introduce observations of one of the parent variables. Consistent with our logical reasoning, we note that if one of the parents (equivalent to causes) of an event is observed, then we have stronger beliefs about the child random variable (*Offer*).

We start by defining a function that reads the JSON data file and creates an object we can use to run probability queries. The following code is from the `Bayes net-Causal Reasoning.ipynb` IPython Notebook:

```
from libpgm.graphskeleton import GraphSkeleton
from libpgm.nodedata import NodeData
from libpgm.discretebayesiannetwork import DiscreteBayesianNetwork
from libpgm.tablecpdfactorization import TableCPDFactorization
def getTableCPD():
    nd = NodeData()
    skel = GraphSkeleton()
    jsonpath="job_interview.txt"
    nd.load(jsonpath)
    skel.load(jsonpath)
    # load bayesian network
    bn = DiscreteBayesianNetwork(skel, nd)
    tablecpd=TableCPDFactorization(bn)
    return tablecpd
```

We can now use the `specificquery` function to run inference queries on the network we have defined. What is the prior probability of getting a $P(\textit{Offer}=1)$ *Offer*? Note that the probability query takes two dictionary arguments: the first one being the query and the second being the evidence set, which is specified by an empty dictionary, as shown in the following code:

```
tcpd=getTableCPD()
tcpd.specificquery(dict(Offer='1'),dict())
```

The following is the output of the preceding code:

```
0.432816
```

It is about 43 percent, and if we now introduce evidence that the candidate has poor grades, how does it change the probability of getting an offer? We will evaluate the value of $P(\textit{Offer}=1 \mid \textit{Grades}=0)$, as shown in the following code:

```
tcpd=getTableCPD()
tcpd.specificquery(dict(Offer='1'),dict(Grades='0'))
```

Directed Graphical Models

The following is the output of the preceding code:

```
0.35148
```

As expected, it decreases the probability of getting an offer since we reason that students with poor grades are unlikely to get an offer. Adding further evidence that the candidate's experience is low as well, we evaluate $P(\mathit{Offer}=1\,|\,\mathit{Grades}=0, \mathit{Experience}=0)$, as shown in the following code:

```
tcpd=getTableCPD()
tcpd.specificquery(dict(Offer='1'),dict(Grades='0',Experience='0'))
```

The following is the output of the preceding code:

```
0.2078
```

As expected, it drops even lower on the additional evidence, from 35 percent to 20 percent.

What we have seen is that the introduction of the observed parent random variable strengthens our beliefs, which leads us to the name causal reasoning.

In the following diagram, we can see the different paths taken by causal and evidential reasoning:

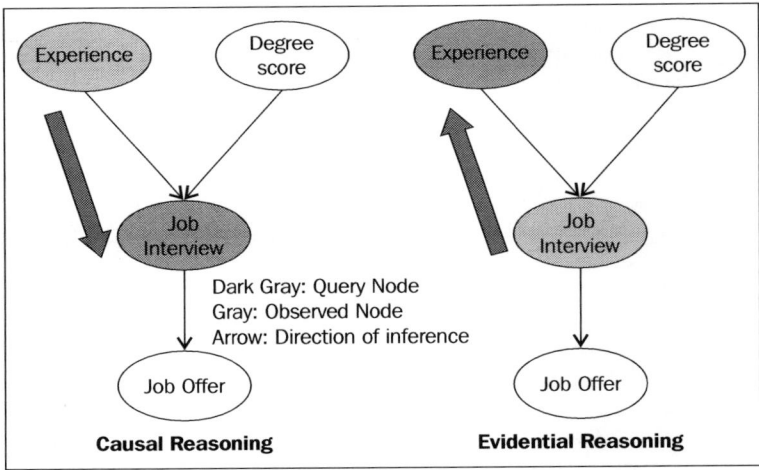

Evidential reasoning

Evidential reasoning is when we observe the value of a child variable, and we wish to reason about how it strengthens our beliefs about its parents. We will evaluate the prior probability of high Experience $P(Experience=1)$, as shown in the following code:

```
tcpd=getTableCPD()
tcpd.specificquery(dict(Experience='1'),dict())
```

The output of the preceding code is as follows:

```
0.4
```

We now introduce evidence that the candidate's interview was good and evaluate the value for *P(Experience=1 | Interview=2)*, as shown in the following code:

```
tcpd=getTableCPD()
print tcpd.specificquery(dict(Experience='1'),dict(Interview='2'))
```

The output of the preceding code is as follows:

```
0.864197530864
```

We see that if the candidate scores well on the interview, the probability that the candidate was highly experienced increases, which follows the reasoning that the candidate must have good experience or education, or both. In evidential reasoning, we reason from effect to cause.

Inter-causal reasoning

Inter-causal reasoning, as the name suggests, is a type of reasoning where multiple causes of a single effect interact. We first determine the prior probability of having high, relevant experience; thus, we will evaluate *P(Experience=1)*, as shown in the following code:

```
tcpd=getTableCPD()
tcpd.specificquery(dict(Experience='1'),dict())
```

The following is the output of the preceding code:

```
0.4
```

By introducing evidence that the interview went extremely well, we think that the candidate must be quite experienced. We will now evaluate the value for $P(Experience = 1 | Interview = 2)$, as shown in the following code:

```
tcpd=getTableCPD()
tcpd.specificquery(dict(Experience='1'),dict(Interview='2'))
```

The following is the output of the preceding code:

```
0.864197530864
```

The Bayes network confirms what we think is true (the candidate is experienced), and the probability of high experience goes up from 0.4 to 0.86. Now, if we introduce evidence that the candidate didn't have good grades and still managed to get a good score in the interview, we may conclude that the candidate must be so experienced that his grades didn't matter at all. We will evaluate the value for $P(Experience = 1 | Interview = 2, Grades = 0)$, as shown in the following code:

```
tcpd=getTableCPD()
tcpd.specificquery(dict(Experience='1'),dict(Interview='2',Grad
es='0'))
```

The output of the preceding code is as follows:

```
0.909090909091
```

This confirms our hunch that even though the probability of high experience went up only a little, it strengthens our belief about the candidate's high experience. This example shows the interplay between the two parents of the **Job interview** node, which are **Experience** and **Degree Score**, and shows us that if we know one of the causes behind an effect, it reduces the importance of the other cause. In other words, we have explained the poor grades on observing the experience of the candidate. This phenomenon is commonly called **explaining away**.

The following diagram shows the path of interaction between nodes involved in inter-causal reasoning:

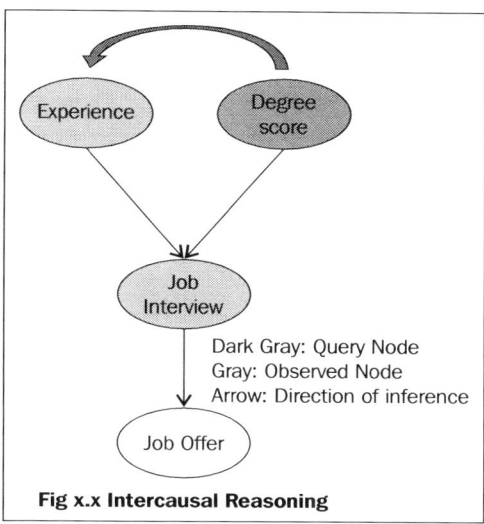

Fig x.x Intercausal Reasoning

Bayes networks are usually drawn with the independent events on top and the influence flows from top to bottom (similar to the job interview example). It may be useful to recall causal reasoning flows from top to bottom, evidential reasoning flows from bottom to top, and inter-causal reasoning flows sideways.

D-separation

Having understood that the direction of arrows indicate that one node can influence another node in a Bayes network, let's see how exactly influence flows in a Bayes network. We can see that the grades eventually influence the job offer, but in the case of a very big Bayes network, it would not help to state that the leaf node is influenced by all the nodes at the top of the Bayes network. Are there conditions where influence does not flow? We shall see that there are simple rules that explain the flow of influence in the following table:

No variables observed	Y has been observed
$X \leftarrow Y \leftarrow Z$ ☺	$X \leftarrow Y \leftarrow$ ☹
$X \rightarrow Y \rightarrow Z$ ☺	$X \rightarrow Y \rightarrow Z$ ☹
$X \leftarrow Y \rightarrow Z$ ☺	$X \leftarrow Y \rightarrow Z$ ☹
$X \rightarrow Y \leftarrow Z$ ☹	$X \rightarrow Y \leftarrow Z$ ☺

Directed Graphical Models

The preceding table depicts the open and closed active trails between three nodes **X**, **Y**, and **Z**. In the first column, no variables are observed, whereas in the second column, **Y** has been observed.

We shall first consider the case where no random variables have been observed. Consider the chains of nodes in the first column of the preceding table. Note that the rules in the first three rows allow the influence to flow from the first to the last node.

Influence can flow along the path of the edges, even if these chains are extended for longer sequences. It must be pointed out that the flow of influence is not restricted by the directionality of the links that connect them.

However, there is one case we should watch out for, which is called the V-structure, $X \to Y \leftarrow Z$ — probably called so because the direction of edges is pointed inwards.

In this case, the influence cannot flow from X to Z since it is blocked by Y. In longer chains, the influence will flow unless it is obstructed by a V-structure.

In this case, $A \to B \to X \leftarrow Y \to Z$ because of the V-structure at X the influence can flow from $A \to B \to X$ and $X \leftarrow Y \to Z$ but not across the node X.

We can now state the concept of an **active trail** (of influence). A trail is active if it contains no V-structures, in the event that no evidence is observed. In case multiple trails exist between two variables, they are conditionally independent if none of the trails are active.

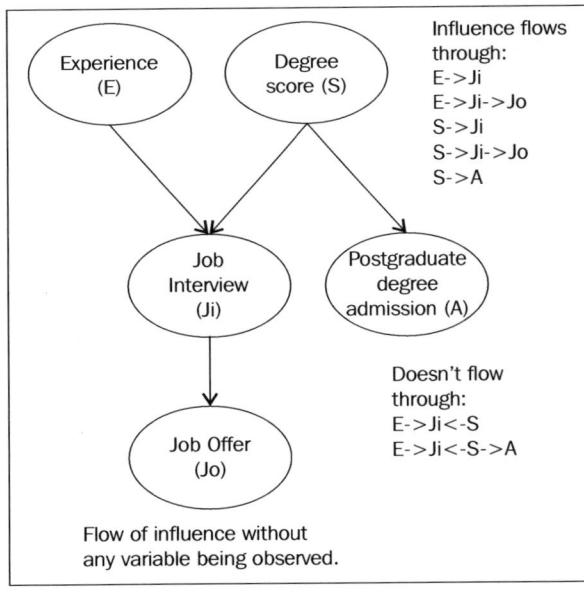

Flow of influence without any variable being observed.

Let's now look at the second case where we do have observed evidence variables. It is easier to understand if we compare the case with the previous chains, where we observe the random variable Y.

The smiley trails shown in the previous table indicate an active trail, and the others indicate a blocked trail. It can be observed that the introduction of evidence simply negates a previously active trail, and it opens up if a previously blocking V-structure existed.

We can now state that a trail given some evidence $\mathbb{Z}$ will be active if the middle node or any of its descendants in any V-structure (for example, Y or its descendants in $X \rightarrow Y \leftarrow Z$) is present in the evidence set $\mathbb{Z}$. In other words, observing Y or any of its children will open up the blocking V-structure, making it an active trail. Additionally, as seen in the the following table, an open trail gets blocked by introduction of evidence and vice versa.

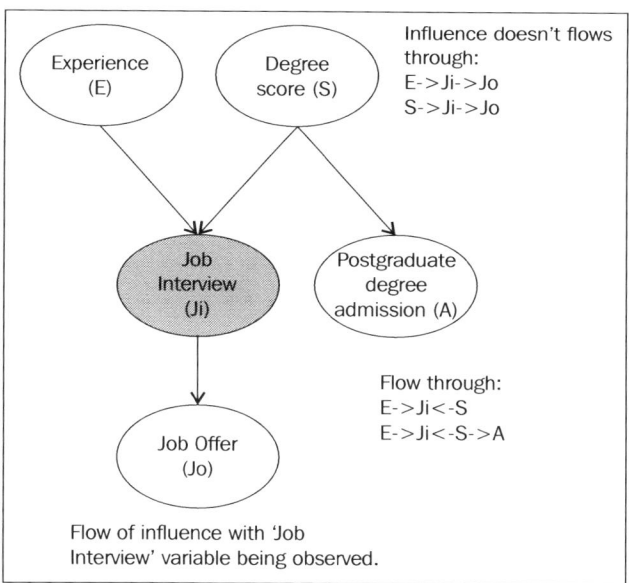

Flow of influence with 'Job Interview' variable being observed.

The D-separation example

In this section, we shall look at using the job candidate example to understand D-separation. In the process of performing causal reasoning, we will query for the job offer and shall introduce the observed variables in the parents of the job offer to verify the concepts of active trails, which we have seen in the previous section. The following code is from the `D-separation.ipynb` IPython Notebook.

Directed Graphical Models

We first query the job offer with no other observed variables, as shown in the following code:

```
getTableCPD().specificquery(dict(Offer='1'),dict())
```

The output of the preceding code is as follows:

```
0.432816
```

We know from the active trail rules that observing `Experience` should change the probability of the offer, as shown in the following code:

```
getTableCPD().specificquery(dict(Offer='1'),dict(Experience='1'))
```

The output of the preceding code is as follows:

```
0.6438
```

As per the output, it changes. Now, let's add the `Interview` observed variable, as shown in the following code:

```
getTableCPD().specificquery(dict(Offer='1'),dict(Interview='1'))
```

The output of the preceding code is as follows:

```
0.6
```

We get a slightly different probability for `Offer`. We know from the D-separation rules that observing `Interview` should block the active trail from `Experience` to `Offer`, as shown in the following code:

```
getTableCPD().specificquery(dict(Offer='1'),dict(Interview='1',Experience='1'))
```

The output of the preceding code is as follows:

```
0.6
```

Observe that the probability of `Offer` does not change from `0.6`, despite the addition of the `Experience` variable being observed. We can add other values of `Interview` object's parent variables, as shown in the following code:

```
query=dict(Offer='1')
results=[getTableCPD().specificquery(query,e) for e in [dict(Interview='1',Experience='0'),
dict(Interview='1',Experience='1'),
dict(Interview='1',Grades='1'),
dict(Interview='1',Grades='0')]]
print results
```

The output of the preceding code is as follows:

```
[0.6, 0.6, 0.6, 0.6]
```

The preceding code shows that once the `Interview` variable is observed, the active trail between `Experience` and `Offer` is blocked. Therefore, `Experience` and `Offer` are conditionally independent when `Interview` is given, which means observing the values of the interview's parents, `Experience` and `Grades`, do not contribute to changing the probability of the offer.

Blocking and unblocking a V-structure

Let's look at the only V-structure in the network, *Experience* → *Interview* ← *Grades*, and see the effect observed evidence has on the active trail.

```
getTableCPD().specificquery(dict(Grades='1'),dict(Experience='0'))
getTableCPD().specificquery(dict(Grades='1'),dict())
```

The result of the preceding code is as follows:

```
0.3
0.3
```

According to the rules of D-separation, the interview node is a V-structure between `Experience` and `Grades`, and it blocks the active trails between them. The preceding code shows that the introduction of the observed variable `Experience` has no effect on the probability of the grades.

```
getTableCPD().specificquery(dict(Grades='1'),dict(Interview='1'))
```

The following is the output of the preceding code:

```
0.413016270338
```

The following code should activate the trail between `Experience` and `Grades`:

```
getTableCPD().specificquery(dict(Grades='1'),dict(Interview='1',Experience='0'))
getTableCPD().specificquery(dict(Grades='1'),dict(Interview='1',Experience='1'))
```

The output of the preceding code is as follows:

```
0.588235294118
0.176470588235
```

The preceding code now shows the existence of an active trail between `Experience` and `Grades`, where changing the observed `Experience` value changes the probability of `Grades`.

Factorization and I-maps

So far, we have understood that a graph G is a representation of a distribution P. We can formally define the relationship between a graph G and a distribution P in the following way.

If G is a graph over random variables $X_1, X_2, \ldots, X_n$, we can state that a distribution P factorizes over G if $P(X_1, X_2, \ldots, X_n) = \prod_i P(X_1 | Par_G(X_i))$. Here, $Par_G(X_i)$ are the parent nodes of X_i. In other words, a joint distribution can be defined as a product of each random variable when its parents are given.

The interplay between factorization and independence is a useful phenomenon that allows us to state that if the distribution factorizes over a graph and given that two nodes $X, Y | Z$ are D-separated, the distribution satisfies those independencies $(X, Y | Z)$.

Alternately, we can state that the graph G is an **Independency map (I-map)** for a distribution P, if P factorizes over G because of which we can read the independencies from the graph, regardless of the parameters. An I-map may not encode all the independencies in the distribution. However, if the graph satisfies all the dependencies in the distribution, it is called a **Perfect map (P-map)**. The graph of the job interview is an example of an I-map.

The Naive Bayes model

We can sum this up by saying that a graph can be seen from the following two viewpoints:

- **Factorization**: This is where a graph allows a distribution to be represented
- **I-map**: This is where the independencies encoded by the graph hold in the distribution

The Naive Bayes model is the one that makes simplistic independence assumptions. We use the Naive Bayes model to perform binary classification Here, we are given a set of instances, where each instance consists of a set of features $X_1, X_2, \ldots, X_n$ and a class y. The task in classification is to predict the correct class of y when the rest of the features $X_1, X_2, \ldots, X_n \ldots$ are given.

For example, we are given a set of newsgroup postings that are drawn from two newsgroups. Given a particular posting, we would like to predict which newsgroup that particular posting was drawn from. Each posting is an instance that consists of a bag of words (we make an assumption that the order of words doesn't matter, just the presence or absence of the words is taken into account), and therefore, the $X_1, X_2, \ldots, X_n$ features indicate the presence or absence of words.

Here, we shall look at the Naive Bayes model as a classifier.

The difference between Naive Bayes and the job candidate example is that Naive Bayes is so called because it makes naïve conditional independence assumptions, and the model factorizes as the product of a prior and individual conditional probabilities, as shown in the following formula:

$$P(C, X_1, X_2, \ldots X_n) = P(C) \prod_{i=2}^{n} P(X_i | C)$$

Although the term on the left is the joint distribution that needs a huge number of independent parameters ($2^{n+1} - 1$ if each feature is a binary value), the Naive Bayes representation on the right needs only 2n+1 parameters, thus reducing the number of parameters from exponential (in a typical joint distribution) to linear (in Naive Bayes).

In the context of the newsgroup example, we have a set of words such as *{atheist, medicine, religion, anatomy}* drawn from the `alt.atheism` and `sci.med` newsgroups. In this model, you could say that the probability of each word appearing is only dependent on the class (that is, the newsgroup) and independent of other words in the posting. Clearly, this is an overly simplified assumption, but it has been shown to have a fairly good performance in domains where the number of features is large and the number of instances is small, such as text classification, which we shall see with a Python program.

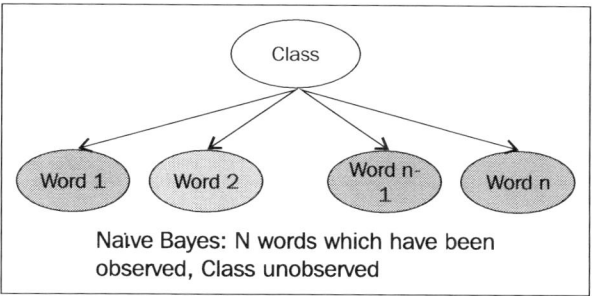

Naive Bayes: N words which have been observed, Class unobserved

Once we see a strong correlation among features, a hierarchical Bayes network can be thought of as an evolved version of a Naive Bayes model.

The Naive Bayes example

In the Naive Bayes example, we will use the Naive Bayes implementation from Scikit-learn—a machine learning library to classify newsgroup postings. We have chosen two newsgroups from the datasets provided by Scikit-learn (alt.atheism and sci.med), and we shall use Naive Bayes to predict which newsgroup a particular posting is from. The following code is from the Naive Bayes.ipynb file:

```
from sklearn.datasets import fetch_20newsgroups
import numpy as np
from sklearn.naive_bayes import MultinomialNB
from sklearn import metrics,cross_validation
from sklearn.feature_extraction.text import TfidfVectorizer
cats = ['alt.atheism', 'sci.med']
newsgroups= fetch_20newsgroups(subset='all',remove=('headers',
'footers', 'quotes'), categories=cats)
```

We first load the newsgroup data using the utility function provided by Scikit-learn (this downloads the dataset from the Internet and may take some time). The newsgroup object is a map, the newsgroup postings are saved against the data key, and the target variables are in newsgroups.target, as shown in the following code:

```
newsgroups.target
```

The output of the preceding code is as follows:

```
array([1, 0, 0, ..., 0, 0, 0], dtype=int64)
```

Since the features are words, we transform them to another representation using **Term Frequency-Inverse Document Frequency (Tfidf)**. The purpose of Tfidf is to de-emphasize words that occur in all postings (such as "the", "by", and "for") and instead emphasize words that are unique to a particular class (such as religion and creationism, which are from the alt.atheism newsgroup). We can do the same by creating a TfidfVectorizer object and then transforming all the newsgroup data to a vector representation, as shown in the following code:

```
vectorizer = TfidfVectorizer()
vectors = vectorizer.fit_transform(newsgroups.data)
```

Vectors now contain features that we can use as the input data to the Naive Bayes classifier. A shape query reveals that it contains 1789 instances, and each instance contains about 24 thousand features, as shown in the following code. However, many of these features can be 0, indicating that the words do not appear in that particular posting:

```
vectors.shape
```

The output of the preceding code is as follows:

```
(1789, 24202)
```

Scikit-learn provides a few versions of the Naive Bayes classifier, and the one we will use is called `MultinomialNB`. Since using a classifier typically involves splitting the dataset into train, test, and validation sets, then training on the train set and testing the efficacy on the validation set, we can use the utility provided by Scikit-learn to do the same for us. The `cross_validation.cross_val_score` function automatically splits the data into multiple sets and returns the `f1` score (a metric that measures a classifier's accuracy), as shown in the following code:

```
clf = MultinomialNB(alpha=.01)
print "CrossValidation Score: ", np.mean(cross_validation.cross_val_score(clf,vectors, newsgroups.target, scoring='f1'))
```

The output of the preceding code is as follows:

```
CrossValidation Score:   0.954618416381
```

We can see that despite the assumption that all features are conditionally independent when the class is given, the classifier maintains a decent `f1` score of 95 percent.

Summary

In this chapter, we learned how conditional independence properties allow a joint distribution to be represented as the Bayes network. We then took a tour of types of reasoning and understood how influence can flow through a Bayes network, and we explored the same concepts using Libpgm. Finally, we used a simple Bayes network (Naive Bayes) to solve a real-world problem of text classification.

In the next chapter, we shall learn about the undirected graphical models or Markov networks.

3
Undirected Graphical Models

We shall now look at models where the interaction between variables is such that the directionality cannot be ascribed to them. We shall see how to represent these undirected models and their properties in terms of their distribution and D-separation.

Pairwise Markov networks

We shall use the following example to motivate our discussions in this chapter. We have four colleagues (**Amar**, **Bob**, **Charlie**, and **Deepak**) who meet at an office party. There's been a rumor at the party that one of the senior managers may leave the organization. These four colleagues bump into each other and have one-on-one conversations, possibly about the rumor. We know that Charlie and Bob bond really well, but the same cannot be said of Charlie and Deepak. In short, each of the pairs influences the other and has a certain amount of like or dislike for each other. We would like the model to capture instances of whether each person either knows or does not know about the rumor. A model of their interactions can be seen in the graph in the following diagram. We will use the Markov network to model whether the four colleagues get to know about the rumor.

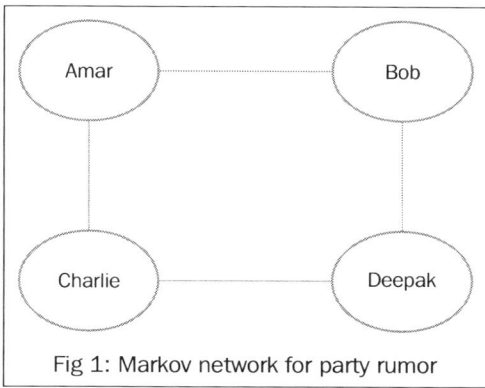

Fig 1: Markov network for party rumor

While modeling the problem, you may recall the Bayesian network, and we can try to model the party example using that. It would appear that the interactions between the variables are symmetric; one cannot ascribe a direction to the affinity between two people. We can model this type of interaction using a Markov network, where the nodes represent random variables and the edges represent affinities, interactions, or likes/dislikes between two nodes.

The interactions between two variables can be represented by a function called a factor, which will quantify the degree of likes or dislikes between the variables in its scope. A factor has a set of input variables called the scope of the factor. The values in a factor are in the set of real numbers, where zero indicates a low affinity and vice versa.

We can represent the preceding network using factors $\phi(A,B)\phi(B,C),\phi(C,D)$, and $\phi(D,A)$, the values of which can be considered as compatibility factors (or local happiness) for Amar and Bob, Bob and Charlie, Charlie and Deepak, and Deepak and Amar, respectively. The values in the following table depict that both Amar and Bob bond quite well and share information, so the possibility of both of them either knowing or not knowing about the rumor is high, and the possibility that one gets to know and doesn't share it with the other person is quite low:

$\phi(A,B)$		
A_0	B_0	20
A_0	B_1	2
A_1	B_0	5
A_1	B_1	10

So, we can see that the graph is broken down into small factors, but how do we define the overall joint distribution? We will do this by using a product of factors defined as follows:

$$\tilde{P}(A,B,C,D) = \phi(A,B) \times \phi(B,C) \times \phi(C,D) \times \phi(D,A)$$

However, you might say, this isn't a valid probability distribution since it doesn't sum up to one, which it rightly doesn't (hence, the tilde $\tilde{p}$). This is rectified by dividing all the terms by Z, which is also called the partition function and is defined as follows:

$$P(A,B,C,D) = \frac{1}{Z}\tilde{P}(A,B,C,D)$$

Here, Z is simply the sum of values in all the factors, as shown in the following formula:

$$Z = \sum_{A,B,C,D} \tilde{P}(A,B,C,D)$$

Since we have learned about the Bayesian network already, a natural question that might arise—is the factor $\phi(A,B)$ some marginal probability $P(A,B)$ or some conditional probability $P(A,B|C,D)$ or some combination thereof? Unfortunately, there isn't direct mapping between those marginal or conditional probabilities and that of a factor. All we can state is that the factor $\phi(A,B)$ is an aggregate of the other factors that comprise the Markov network. Consequently, there is no direct mapping between the probability distributions encoded by the Markov network and the factors that the network is composed of, which is a little different from what we've encountered in the Bayesian network.

We can define a pairwise Markov network as an undirected graph composed of nodes that represent random variables $X_1, X_2, \ldots X_n$, which are connected by edges between two nodes $(X_a \to X_b)$. This indicates the factor (or potential) between the two nodes, that is, $\phi_{ab}(A,B)$.

The Gibbs distribution

In the pairwise Markov network, our factors had only two variables in its scope. If we expanded the network so that each node connects to all other nodes in the network, we would get edges as in the following diagram:

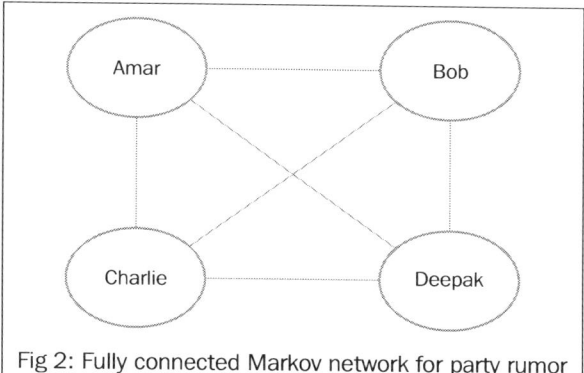

Fig 2: Fully connected Markov network for party rumor

Undirected Graphical Models

Would P(A, B, C, D) from a pairwise Markov network represent any probability distribution over random variables A, B, C, D? No, because the parameters in this network are not enough to describe a joint probability distribution over n random variables (which would need d^n parameters, if each random variable takes on d values). An observant reader might have noticed that for the preceding pairwise Markov network (with four variables), the number of parameters (as compared to the joint distribution) are indeed equal. Let's look at the following table for the number of parameters required when each random variable takes binary values:

Number of random variables	Number of edges (factors)	Parameters in a pairwise Markov network	Parameters in a joint distribution (d^n)
4 (2 x 2 grid)	4	16	2^4=16
9 (3 x 3 grid)	12	48	2^9=512

We can see that, in a general case, the number of parameters in a pairwise Markov network is insufficient to represent a joint distribution. One way out of this problem is to allow a ϕ factor to have an unlimited number of variables in its scope, unlike just two in a pairwise case. This is called a Gibbs distribution and is defined as follows:

$$\Phi = \{\phi_1(D_1), \phi_2(D_2)..\phi_k(D_k)\}$$

Each ϕ_i factor might have several variables in its scope (D_i), and the Gibbs distribution is a set of such factors. Just as we have seen for the pairwise case, the unnormalized distribution is a product of its factors, as shown in the following formula:

$$\tilde{P}(X_1,..X_n) = \prod_{i=1}^{k} \phi_i(D_i)$$

And to make it a probability distribution that sums up to 1 (since factors are not constrained in the values they can take), we have to normalize by dividing it by the partition function Z. We get $P(X_1,..X_n) = \frac{1}{Z_\phi} \prod_{i=1}^{k} \phi_i(D_i)$, where Z_ϕ is $\sum_{X_1..X_n} \tilde{P}(X_1,..X_n)$.

So, what does this Gibbs distribution really give us? It simply gives us a valid probability distribution (that sums up to 1), and it seems similar to a probability distribution that could be mapped to a graph as in a Bayesian network.

An induced Markov network

What would the Markov network look like if we have factors that involve multiple variables? In the pairwise case, the $\phi(A,B)$ factor meant an edge between random variables A and B. It is indeed logical to assume that the $\phi(A,B,C)$ factor would have an edge among all the pairs. This is called an **Induced Markov network**, where the figure contains edges for the two factors $\phi(A,B,C)$ and $\phi(B,C,D)$, which can be seen in the following diagram:

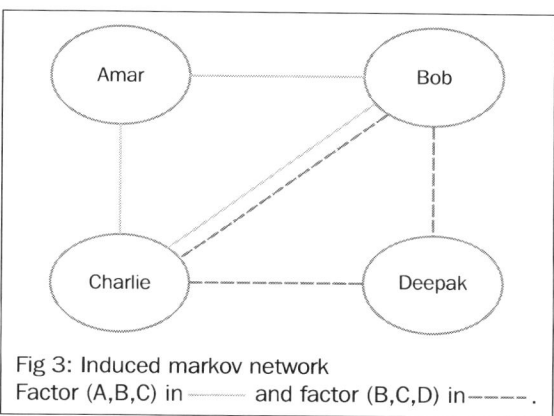

Fig 3: Induced markov network
Factor (A,B,C) in ——— and factor (B,C,D) in -----.

Factorization

Throughout the representation section of the Bayesian network, we have encountered two representations: one being a graph, and the other being a probability distribution. We asked ourselves questions such as are they equivalent and when we switch from one view to the other, do we lose or gain information? We will now examine these questions in the context of a Markov network.

What is the equivalency of a distribution D and graph G? When does D factorize over G? In other words, when can D be represented using G? One way to understand factorization is to think of it as a decomposition problem. We have a problem (a huge joint distribution, for example), and we want to decompose it into smaller pieces (such as conditional probability distributions in the case of the Bayesian network).

We can state that the distribution D factorizes over G if we have a set of factors Φ (which is a product of its individual factors), and that G is the induced graph for the set of factors Φ.

Undirected Graphical Models

Unlike in the Bayesian network, however, if we are given a graph G, there is no single unique set of factors that can be read from the graph. Let's take a look at the following diagram:

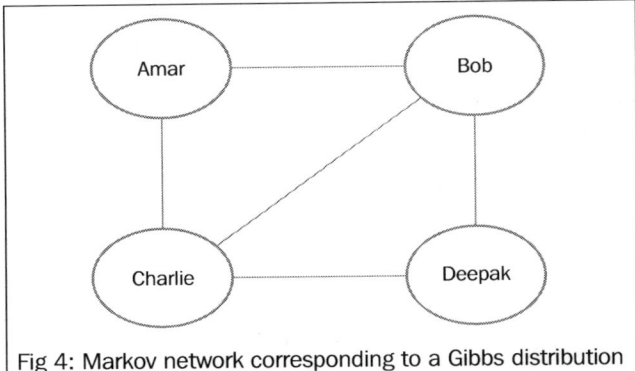

Fig 4: Markov network corresponding to a Gibbs distribution

We know that all (pairs of) variables in the scope of a factor are connected by edges. For example, in the $\phi_2(B,C,D)$ factor, there's an edge between $(B,C), (C,D)$ and (B,D). The same is true for all the other factors.

Now consider two sets of factors: $S_1 : \{\phi_1(A,B,C), \phi_2(B,C,D)\}$ and $S_2 : \{\phi_1(A,B,C), \phi_2(C,D), \phi_3(B,D)\}$. We can see that in both sets, each individual factor satisfies the condition that all the variables in its scope are connected by an edge. If we were to draw a diagram with the four vertices A, B, C, D and then connect the edges as described by the factor set S_1 or S_2, we would find the diagram that materializes is the same.

Therefore, different sets of factors can induce the same graph, and the factorization, or splitting into individual factors, cannot be read from the graph. That should not be read as not good enough compared to the Bayesian network, but that a graph can have multiple factorizations, all of which are correct.

Flow of influence

How does influence flow along a Markov network? We have already seen that there is no single unique factorization in a given graph G, and the flow of influence doesn't depend on the form of the factors.

Two variables can influence each other as long as they are connected through a set of edges. In the preceding diagram, **Amar**, **Bob**, and **Charlie** are connected through a set of edges and can influence each other, and the factorization, whether $\phi_1(A,B,C)$ or $\{\phi_1(A,B), \phi_2(B,C)\}$, doesn't really matter.

Active trail and separation

Unlike the detailed rules of active trails in Bayesian networks, in Markov networks, the rule is simple: an influence can flow between any two random variables that are connected by edges. A node is blocked if it has been observed. We can see this in the example in the following diagram.

We can thus state the concept of separation in Markov networks (note that we don't call it D-separation because this is not a directed graph). The random variables X and Y, given the evidence set Z, are separated in a graph G if there is no active trail in G between X and Y. That is, there should be no evidence or observed nodes in one of the trails that connects X and Y.

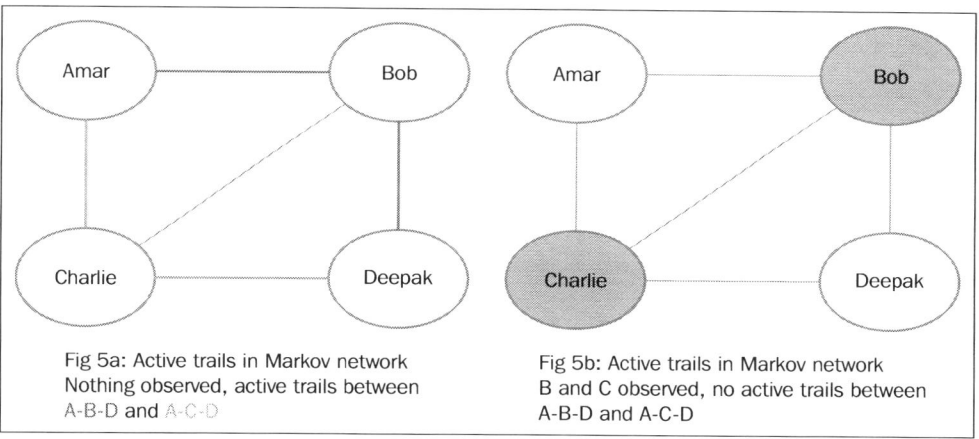

Fig 5a: Active trails in Markov network
Nothing observed, active trails between
A-B-D and A-C-D

Fig 5b: Active trails in Markov network
B and C observed, no active trails between
A-B-D and A-C-D

Structured prediction

In typical applications of machine learning classifiers, the classifier predicts a class for the target variable, such as spam/non-spam to classify an e-mail. Usually, each instance (such as an individual e-mail) is independent of the next or previous e-mail.

However, there are several classes of applications where the target variable is related to its neighbors. Take the case of image segmentation where a typical problem is that in a picture of a cow on a pasture, we want to classify each pixel (or super pixel, which is a contiguous group of pixels as described by the image processing literature) as cow or grass. Each super pixel has a few neighbors, and if the super pixel Sp is at the stomach region of the cow and surrounded by other super pixels already classified as cow, it is quite obvious that the super pixel Sp should also be classified as cow. The task of classifying the super pixel Sp is made much easier by using the local structure rather than by classifying it independently, ignoring the nearby super pixels.

Similarly, in the field of natural language processing, the task called **Part of Speech tagging (POS tagging)** involves tagging each word in a sentence with a word category such as noun, pronoun, or verb. Here too, tagging a word as a noun or a verb is much easier if we look at the whole sentence rather than each word in isolation.

In such cases, where we wish to perform task-specific prediction, and there exists a local structure that we can exploit, we can use models such as **Hidden Markov Models (HMMs)** and **Conditional Random Fields (CRFs)**. The local structure can be words located nearby in a sequence of words or pixels situated nearby in a grid of pixels.

Problem of correlated features

If we are trying to predict the class of super pixels, the features (such as the color histogram for each super pixel) are highly correlated with each other. In a generative model such as Naive Bayes, the same feature gets counted multiple times, which gives a highly skewed probability towards a class. Correcting the independence assumptions requires adding edges between features because features that are correlated are not conditionally independent. It is hard to figure out how they are correlated, and the models get densely connected, which means lots of edges between lots of vertices.

One solution to this problem is to model $Y|X$ instead of (X,Y), that is, model the conditional distribution instead of the joint distribution (where Y is the set of target variables, and X is the set of observed variables). We aren't concerned about how the features vary (or don't vary together); we only care about the target variable. A CRF differs from an MRF by trying to model the conditional distribution $Y|X$ rather than the joint distribution (X,Y).

The CRF representation

A CRF can be represented by a set of factors $\Phi = \{\phi_1(D_1), \phi_2(D_2)..\phi_k(D_k)\}$, which seems similar to the Gibbs distribution. The difference is that the normalization constant Z only sums over all the values of Y.

If the joint distribution has two variables A and B, as shown in the following formula:

$$\tilde{P}(A,B) = \prod_{i=1}^{k} \phi_i(D_i)$$

Then, the conditional distribution is normalized by dividing by z_a, as shown in the following formula:

$$P(B \mid A) = \frac{1}{Z_a} \tilde{P}(A, B)$$

Here, $Z_a = \sum_a \tilde{P}(A,B)$ is the joint distribution with the values for A, summed out.

The Naive Bayes model is an example of a generative model (the one that models the joint distribution), and the conditional equivalent of it is a logistic regression model (one that models the conditional distribution).

The CRF example

The use of CRFs can be understood better with this example:

Given a set of images that correspond to handwritten characters in words, we need to predict the character in each image. We can imagine that the solution we build will start with the simplest possible one, and then work toward improving it. The simplest model we can start with is the one that has singleton factors, that is, each character's predicted value will depend only on the image features, as depicted in the following diagram. The images **I1** to **I4** have been observed, and we want to recognize the class variables **c1** to **c4** (which can take on 26 values, one for each character from A to Z).

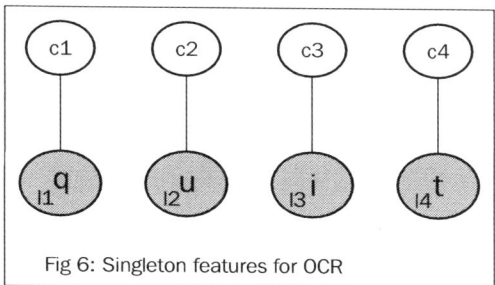

Fig 6: Singleton features for OCR

We can get fairly good predictive scores using the singleton features by using a strong classifier such as logistic regression or random forests.

However, we can see that this model can be improved. Consider the character I2 in the previous diagram. We know that the most common character following the letter **q** is **u**, and the other characters are extremely uncommon. Similarly, the characters that follow **qui** are likely to be **t** or **d** (quid or quit). We can encode knowledge by adding pairwise features (between two character classes), triplet features (between three character classes), or even more. Observe the following diagram that depicts edges for the added features:

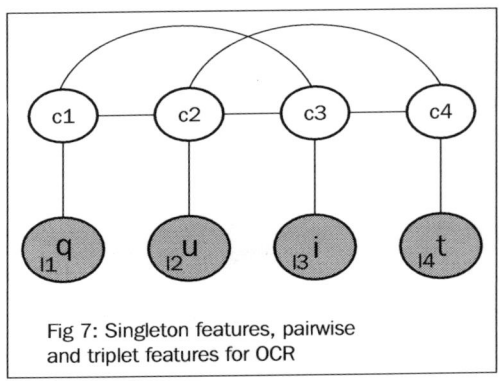

Fig 7: Singleton features, pairwise and triplet features for OCR

The singleton factors that capture the potential between the class C and the image I can be represented as $\phi_i(C_i, I_i)$, and the pairwise and triplet factors can be represented as $\phi_i(C_i, C_{i+1})$ and $\phi_i(C_i, C_{i+1}, C_{i+2})$. The pairwise features for English characters would be for all combinations such as {A - A}, {A - B}, {A - C} all the way up to {Z - Z}, and similarly for the triplet factors {A - A A}, {A - A B}, and so on. Given that we have 26 characters in English, we will need 26^2 and 26^3 factors, respectively, to represent all the combinations for pairwise and triplet factors. We have to learn the parameters for these factors from the data. For example, to learn the parameters for {X-Y-Z}, we can count the number of occurrences of the characters {X-Y-Z} in a large corpus of words. We might expect that many of such factors occur extremely rarely (for example, the combination *xmq*).

It may be tempting to add larger factors that have more than three variables in its scope, but given the exponential growth, it becomes difficult to store, manipulate, and run inference on a network with an exponential number of factors.

The factorization-independence tango

In the previous chapter, we understood that the two concepts of a graph and a distribution are both encoded in a graphical model. We now turn to the equivalence of factorization and independence, and we would like to know whether they are both respected in both the views, in the context of Markov nets.

The following are the questions that we wish to address:

- The first one is if the two nodes are conditionally independent in the graph, does the distribution respect that independence?
- The second one is that is the factorization (or decomposition) of a distribution into a graph a valid decomposition?

This is a theorem that has parallels from Bayesian networks. If a distribution P factorizes over a graph G, and suppose that two random variables X and Y are separated (in the graph G) given $\phi_i(C_i, C_{i+1}, C_{i+2})$, then the distribution P satisfies the independence statement, and X is conditionally independent of Y given Z.

In other words, the independence defined by the graph H by the separation properties is preserved by the distribution P that represents the graph. Similar to the Bayesian network, the graph H is an I-map of the distribution P.

The converse of this relationship is independence of factorization—if the distribution P satisfies the independencies described by the graph G, P factorizes over the graph G. Unlike the case of the Bayesian network, this is true only for positive distributions, that is, the probabilities have to be greater than zero for all assignments to the random variables. This relationship follows from the Hammersley-Clifford theorem.

To sum up, just as in the case of the Bayesian network, we have two equivalent views of the Markov network. Factorization enables a graph G to represent a (positive) distribution, and I-map enables the independencies described by the graph G to be respected in the (positive) distribution.

Summary

In this chapter, we learned about Markov random fields, which are an alternative representation of graphical models. We learned about their properties, their similarities, and dissimilarities with Bayesian networks. We also looked at some real-world applications where MRFs are being used. We also learned about conditional random fields and how they can be used for structured prediction.

Having learned the concepts and means to represent PGMs, in the next part of the book, we shall learn how to convert representations to artifacts that can be consumed by software tools to solve real-world problems.

4
Structure Learning

The common path we may take while using a PGM to solve a problem is that we start with a dataset, and then we run some types of inference queries on this dataset. We may have some domain knowledge of the structure of the network, as well as the knowledge of the parameters of this network. Often times, we may not have prior knowledge of either the network structure or parameter priors, and all that we have is a dataset.

Given a dataset, we have the following tasks at hand:

- Learn the structure of the network. This can be achieved by learning from the data alone, or by also providing some domain knowledge (of connections between edges).
- Learn the parameters of the network. Again, domain knowledge can help us with parameter priors, or it can be learned entirely from data.
- Use an inference engine to run conditional probability queries or MAP queries.

There is an implicit need for a tool that can help us do all of the preceding tasks, structure and parameter learning, as well as inference.

In the next part of the book, we will explore structure, parameter learning, and finally inference, in the same order.

In this chapter, we will learn how to learn the structure of a PGM.

When we wish to use a PGM, one task is to determine the structure of the graphical model. Sometimes, we have a domain expert who can arrange a suitable hierarchical model. Unfortunately, this is not always the case, and we may want to learn the structure of the network given the data without any prior domain knowledge. Even with some domain expertise available, we would like to verify or improve the structure of the network.

Another use of structure learning is when the goal is to discover the structure (and not necessarily discover it just to run inference queries). For example, causal Bayesian networks have been used to model protein signaling networks, where discovering the network structure is applied to understand drug interactions and dysfunctional signaling in diseased cells.

The structure learning landscape

The tour of structure learning goes in this fashion: the algorithms that we discuss can be divided into two areas, one that uses constraints and the other that focuses on score-based approaches.

We will also discuss the kind of structures that are found, such as trees, forests, and graphs. We will explore the pros and cons of algorithms in each set, and also try out some simple examples that exercise some algorithms.

Constraint-based structure learning

In this approach, we start with a set of vertices that represent random variables in the data, and then we test for conditional dependence (and independence) in the data. The goal of this approach is to read the conditional dependence and independence of the data from the Bayesian network structure. The constraints are essentially tests of conditional independencies between the random variables.

The algorithm can be logically divided into three parts.

Part I

For each variable X_i, the algorithm attempts to find a subset of witness variables (say, X_1 to X_n) in the presence of which X_i is independent of the other variables. However, examining all subsets of the random variables will require searching over an exponential number. To remedy this, the algorithm uses only a polynomial number of independence tests by doing the following task:

It restricts the number of parents for each vertex. This depends on our intuition about the size of the network. A larger network may need a larger subset of witness variables.

The procedure used to determine conditional independence also merits some discussion. This problem is commonly solved in statistics literature using hypothesis testing. Assuming that we have a distribution over variables A and B, we wish to know whether the joint distribution is the product of individual probabilities, $P(A,B)=P(A)P(B)$. A distribution where the variables are not independent may be $P(A,B)=P(A)P(B|A)$.

A suitable test to accept or reject the null hypothesis (the null hypothesis states that the two variables are independent), for discrete valued random variables, is the chi-squared test. The chi-squared test is likely to return a value of 0 when two variables are independent, and it will return a high value when they are not. The Pearson chi-square test statistic is calculated by using the following formula:

$$x^2 = \sum_{i=1}^{n} \frac{(O_i - E_i)^2}{E_i}$$

In this formula, the parameters are as follows:

- x^2: This is the Pearson cumulative test statistic
- O_i: This is the observed frequency
- E_i: This is the expected or theoretical frequency given by the null hypothesis
- n: This is the degree of freedom

With the chi-squared test, we can build a set of independencies in the network. However, when running multiple hypothesis tests, statistical errors can accumulate and result in incorrect independence assumptions due to sparse data as well as statistical noise. On a small network with a large number of instances, these errors will not affect the correctness of the structure, but this cannot be said for a large network. A large network with insufficient data may have spurious independencies generated, which will result in an incorrect structure being built.

Part II

It is known that the graph of independencies (I-map) in a distribution P is not unique, which means that there are multiple graphs G* that can represent the distribution, and these graphs can be called I-equivalent. The goal of this algorithm is to find any one network that is a member of the I-equivalent class of G*.

Structure Learning

In the second part, we will create an undirected graph or a graph skeleton where we add edges between X and Y nodes if they are adjacent in the graph. By adjacency, we mean that the final graph will have a directed edge of the form $X \rightarrow Y$ or $X \leftarrow Y$. We can use independence queries of the form $X \perp Y | U$ to conclude if they are adjacent. If we find any witness nodes U, it will block the active trail between X and Y, leading to the conclusion that X and Y are conditionally independent. On the other hand, if we do not find any witness nodes U, we conclude that they must be conditionally dependent and therefore we add an edge that connects X and Y.

Given that we have a set of independencies, we add edges between the nodes that are not independent using the tests mentioned previously.

Part III

Now that we have a skeleton, we wish to convert the undirected edges into directed edges. A theorem (Koller 3.8) posits that all directed graphs that are I-equivalent to G* have the same set of immoralities. Assume a node has two parents; the parents are immoral if they are not connected by an edge (possibly an analogy to being unmarried). The algorithm proceeds to test and verify potential immoralities in the skeleton. The potential immorality, which is currently represented as $X - Z - Y$, has to change to one of the following ones:

- $X \rightarrow Z \rightarrow Y$
- $X \leftarrow Z \leftarrow Y$
- $X \rightarrow Z \leftarrow Y$
- $X \leftarrow Z \rightarrow Y$

For each of these four destinations, we have the rules that determine the correct destination given an undirected triplet of nodes. For a description of the rules, please refer to Koller 3.4.3.2 onwards.

We will now look at the `constraint-based.ipynb` IPython Notebook, where we attempt to learn the structure of a Bayesian network by using constraint-based approaches. We will first load the network, as shown in the following code:

```
from libpgm.nodedata importNodeData
from libpgm.graphskeleton importGraphSkeleton
from libpgm.discretebayesiannetwork importDiscreteBayesianNetwork
from libpgm.pgmlearner importPGMLearner

nd=NodeData()
skel=GraphSkeleton()
```

```
fpath="job_interview.txt"
nd.load(fpath)
skel.load(fpath)
skel.toporder()
bn=DiscreteBayesianNetwork(skel,nd)
```

It may seem strange that we are loading a network with existing structure and parameters (which are defined in the `job_interview.txt` file). For this example, we will be using synthetic data, which are the samples drawn from an existing network. This helps us compare our results with the known network that we started with. To start with, we will draw two random samples from the `job_interview` network, which we have seen in the previous chapters, as shown in the following code:

```
bn.randomsample(2)
```

The output of the preceding code is as follows:

```
[{u'Admission': u'admitted',
u'Experience': u'high',
u'Grades': u'poor',
u'Interview': u'good',
u'Offer': u'no'},
 {u'Admission': u'admitted',
u'Experience': u'low',
u'Grades': u'poor',
u'Interview': u'poor',
u'Offer': u'yes'}]
```

We can see that the random sample is one specific assignment to each random variable, which is drawn from the joint distribution. It could also be thought of as a random assignment for all the nodes in the network.

Let's discuss how the algorithm proceeds. We first inquire about the conditional independence of all pairs of nodes. This is achieved by running the chi-squared test. The null hypothesis states that nodes X and Y are conditionally independent, given Z.

The following `discrete_condind` method returns the value of chi-square as well as the p-values, which is the probability that the independence is due to chance. We choose a threshold value for the p-value (say, 0.05). If the chi-square test statistic returns a p-value greater than the threshold, it means that the probability of independence between X and Y is too high to have occurred by chance. So, we can conclude that X and Y are indeed independent.

```
learner = PGMLearner()
data = bn.randomsample(200)
X,Y='Grades','Offer'
```

Structure Learning

```
c,p,w=learner.discrete_condind(data,X,Y,[])
print "independence between X and Y: ",c," p-value",p," witness node:
",w
```

The output of the preceding code is as follows:

```
independence between X and Y:    8184619.56996   p-value 0.0
witness node:    []
```

We will run independence queries from the job interview network described in the following diagram:

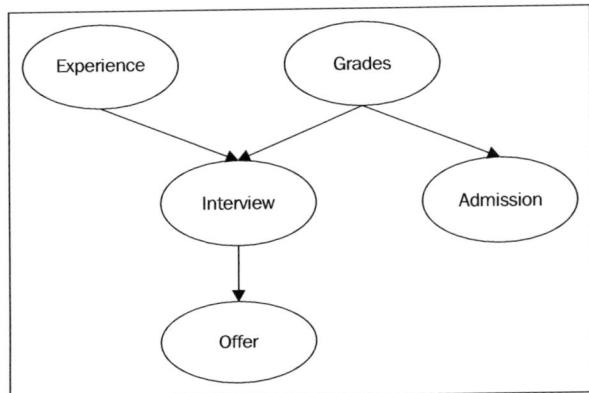

In the query from the preceding code snippet, we can see that the p-value is less than 0.05, and the `Grades` and `Offer` variables can be considered not independent. Since the D-separation rules state that given the job interview network, `Grades` and `Offer` have an active trail between them, which gets blocked if the `Interview` variable is observed. What happens if we observe the `Interview` variable that lies between `Grades` and `Offer`?:

```
X,Y='Grades','Offer'
c,p,w=learner.discrete_condind(data,X,Y,['Interview'])
print "Independence between X and Y: ",c," p-value",p," witness node
",w
```

The output of the preceding code is as follows:

Now, `Grades` and `Offer` are conditionally independent (because the p-value is much greater than 0.05). The first stage of the algorithm essentially tries to determine the conditional independence for all the pairs of nodes in the network, given other witness variables. We are then left with a set of undirected dependencies between nodes.

```
Independence between X and Y:   2.79444519518    p-value 0.993172910586
witness node   ['Interview']
```

The second and third stages of the algorithm are essentially contained in the `discrete_constraint_estimatestruct` method, where the set of dependencies are converted into an undirected graph. Then, the directionalities are resolved. This is shown in the following code:

```
result=learner.discrete_constraint_estimatestruct(data)
print result.E
```

The output of the preceding code is as follows:

```
[[u'Grades', u'Admission'], [u'Experience', u'Interview'], [u'Grades',
u'Interview'], [u'Interview', u'Offer']]
```

The `result.E` variable returns the directed edges learned in the network, and each edge is a list containing the starting and finishing node for the edge. We can see that the four original edges in the job interview network have been found. However, this is a small network. Will this algorithm scale to a larger network?

We will now look at the `alarm_network.ipynb` IPython Notebook, in which we attempt constraint-based approaches on a larger dataset. The logical alarm reduction mechanism network is a Bayesian network designed to provide an alarm message system to monitor patients. This network has 37 vertices and 46 edges, considerably larger than the job interview network we have been using so far, which had 5 vertices and 4 edges.

The dataset can be found at http://www.cs.ru.nl/~peterl/BN/alarm.csv and is commonly referred to as the alarm network. More information on the dataset (such as column descriptions) can be found at http://www.bnlearn.com/documentation/man/alarm.html.

Let us load the `alarm.csv` file by using the `pandas` library, as shown in the following code:

```
import pandas as pd
import numpy as np
df=pd.read_csv("alarm.csv")
```

The `alarm.csv` file has records that we should convert into a format that `libpgm` can consume. Each instance should be a dictionary, where keys are column names and values are column values. The following function performs the format conversion and returns a list of dictionaries that are sampled without replacement from the original dataset. This is shown in the following code:

```
from random import randint,sample

def rand_index(dframe,n_samples=100):
```

Structure Learning

```
    rindex =  np.array(sample(xrange(len(dframe))) ,n_samples if n_
samples<=len(dframe) else len(dframe)))
    return [{i:j.values()[0] for i,j in dframe.iloc[[k]].to_dict().
items()} for k in rindex ]

#Lets examine a single sample:
rand_index(df,n_samples=1)
```

The preceding code gives the following output:

```
[{'Anaphylaxis': 'b',
 'ArtCOb': 'b',
 'BP': 'c',
 'CO': 'a',
 'CVP': 'a',
  ….<rows elided>
}]
```

Let's load the data, create an instance of the learner object, and estimate the structure with a small number of samples (100), as shown in the following code:

```
from libpgm.nodedata import NodeData
from libpgm.graphskeleton import GraphSkeleton
from libpgm.discretebayesiannetwork import DiscreteBayesianNetwork
from libpgm.pgmlearner import PGMLearner

data=rand_index(df,n_samples=100)
learner = PGMLearner()
result=learner.discrete_constraint_estimatestruct(data)
print result.E
```

The output of the preceding code is as follows:

```
[['VentLung', 'MinVol'], ['HR', 'HRBP'], ['LVFailure', 'History'],
['BP', 'TPR'], ['SaOb', 'Shunt'], ['Intubation', 'Shunt'], ['PCWP',
'LVEDVolume'], ['Hypovolemia', 'LVEDVolume']]
```

To compare the performance of the structure learned by libpgm with the correct alarm network, let's load the correct alarm network described in the parent-child.txt file. Each line of this file contains the parent vertex, followed by the child vertices (in some cases, some nodes are leaf nodes that have no children). This is shown in the following code:

```
file = open('parent-child.txt', 'r')

def edges(line):
```

```
    st=line.strip('\n').strip(' ').split(' ')
    #print st
    return [[st[0],i] for i in st[1:] ]

all_edges=[l for line in file for l in edges(line)]
#a set containing the correct edges
ground_truth=set([tuple(i) for i in all_edges])
print all_edges[:5]
```

The output of the preceding code is as follows:

```
[['HISTORY', 'LVFAILURE'], ['CVP', 'LVEDVOLUME'], ['PCWP', 'LVEDVOLUME'],
['LVEDVOLUME', 'HYPOVOLEMIA'], ['LVEDVOLUME', 'LVFAILURE']]
```

Let's define a diagnostic function that compares the found network with the correct network. We wish to enquire about the number of edges in both, as well as the number of edges with right directedness and the edges that connect nodes correctly but have wrong directionality. The code is as follows:

```
def printdiag(result):
    found=set([tuple([j.upper() for j in i]) for i in result.E])
    correct=ground_truth.intersection(found)
    undirected_common_edges=[(i,j) for i,j in found for k,l in
    ground_truth if i.find(k)!=-1 and j.find(l)!=-1]
    print "Number of edges in learnt network ",len(found)
    print "Total number of edges in true network ",len(ground_truth)
    print "Number of edges with correct directionality ",len(correct)
    print "Number of edges with incorrect directionality
",len(undirected_common_edges)
```

Let's define a function that prints the resulting statistics when the dataset picks a specific number of samples as follows:

```
def learn_structure(n_samples):
    data=rand_index(df,n_samples)
    learner = PGMLearner()

result1=learner.discrete_constraint_estimatestruct(data)
printdiag(result1)

learn_structure(1000)
```

The output of the preceding code is as follows:

```
Number of edges in learnt   36
Total number of edges in true network   46
Number of edges with correct directionality   6
Number of edges with incorrect directionality   7
```

Let's examine the performance of the `learn_structure` method when provided with 1000 samples, as shown in the following code. It finds less than half of the edges, and only a few edges correctly connect nodes. Does increasing the sample size help? (This may take a few minutes to run.):

```
learn_structure(10000)
```

The output of the preceding code is as follows:

```
Number of edges in learnt network    30
Total number of edges in true network    46
Number of edges with correct directionality    2
Number of edges with incorrect directionality    3
```

We can see that the number of samples is still not enough to improve the number of edges that are correctly identified. It is not surprising that the algorithm did not learn the correct structure, since the complexity grows exponentially. The number of nodes feasible for exact methods is said to be about 30 (Cassio de Campos, ICML 2009). The complexity of the algorithm has a running time of $O(n^{d+2})$ where n is the number of vertices and d is the upper bound on the witness set. Various versions of this algorithm try to constrain the witness set to improve its performance (this is described in *Chapter 2, Directed Graphical Models* (http://arxiv.org/pdf/1111.6925.pdf)).

Summary of constraint-based approaches

The constraint-based approach is a method that can learn the structure for both directed and undirected graphical models. These methods are quite sensitive to noise in the data, which can give rise to the mistaken independence assumptions and cause the network to miss out on finding the I-equivalent structure. They do not scale to networks with large number of nodes, which can be improved by setting the bounds to the size of the witness set.

Score-based learning

A score-based approach is one that assigns a score that indicates how well a graph fits the data and then searches over the space of all the possible network structures to find a graph that maximizes the score. The score-based approaches enforce sparsity (fewer edges). This causes an optimization problem, where we have an exponential number of network structures to search over.

The likelihood score

The likelihood score is a score that maximizes the likelihood of the data, given a particular graph structure G. The maximum likelihood estimates the parameters of G. Often, the log of the likelihood score is used. The likelihood score decomposes to the following formula:

$$score_l(G:D) = M\sum_{i=1}^{n} I_{\hat{p}}(X_i; Pa_{X_i}^G) - M\sum_{i} H_{\hat{p}}(X_i)$$

The right-hand side of the equation consists of two terms:

The first term $M\sum_{i=1}^{n} I_{\hat{p}}(X_i; Pa_{X_i}^G)$ is the sum over mutual information (denoted by $I_{\hat{p}}$) between a node X_i and its parents $Pa_{X_i}^G$ in the graph. Mutual information is an information-theoretic criterion that can be understood as the average distance between the joint distribution $P(X_1, X_2)$ and the product of marginal distributions $P(X_1) \times P(X_2)$ for two random variables X_1 and X_2.

The second term $M\sum_{i} H_{\hat{p}}(X_i)$ is the sum of entropy of each random variable. It may be observed that it is independent of its parents (and thus independent of the graph structure). M is the number of samples.

The intuition behind the likelihood score is that a network's structure is better if a variable is correlated with its parents. In other words, a graph with a better score will put a variable and its parents together.

Let's compare the scores obtained for the simple network involving two random variables, as shown in the following diagram:

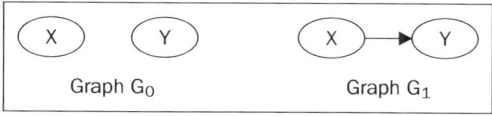

To compare scores between the two networks, we can subtract their scores (using the previous equation).

We can see that when we subtract the scores, the (second) entropy term cancels out, leaving only the first term $I_{\hat{p}}(X;Y)$, which is the mutual information between X and Y. This is shown in the following formula:

$$G_0 - G_1 = MI_{\hat{p}}(X;Y)$$

The mutual information score is always greater than or equal to zero. When two random variables X and Y are independent, the mutual information should be zero. However, in the real world where we may encounter statistical noise in the dataset, given enough samples, there will always be some dependence between random variables resulting in a nonzero value of mutual information.

Why is this important to us? It is important because the mutual information term rewards a network for adding an edge and seldom for removing an edge, and thus the resulting networks that are densely connected get higher scores than sparsely connected networks.

This phenomenon is known as overfitting, and as we know from the machine learning literature, it is something to avoid (because it complicates parameter learning in a PGM). The methods to avoid overfitting can involve restricting the number of parents and parameters. Other scoring functions (which we will see in the further sections) have provisions to penalize overfitting and can build a tradeoff between a network that is connected enough and its fit to the data.

The Bayesian information criterion score

Scoring functions that try to improve on the likelihood score try to penalize complexity in various ways. The **Bayesian information criterion** (**BIC**) and the **Akaike information criterion** (**AIC**) are information-theoretic scores that measure that quality of a statistical model's fit to the data. The approach the BIC score takes is that it subtracts a penalty term (the second term in the following equation) from the likelihood (the first term), as shown in the following formula:

$$score_{BIC}(G:D) = \ell(\theta_g : D) - \frac{\log M}{2} Dim[G]$$

Here, M is the number of training instances and $Dim[G]$ is the number of independent parameters in the distribution (in a joint distribution, the number of independent parameters is the total number of rows in the joint distribution minus one). The second term tries to restrict the likelihood term's propensity to add edges as a function of the number of parameters and training instances.

The second term is just one approach to balance the tradeoff between model complexity and its fit to data. If the $\frac{\log M}{2}$ is replaced by 1, it is called AIC. The negation of the BIC score is called the **Minimum description length** (**MDL**) criterion.

It has been shown that the BIC score has a property called consistency. As the number of data instances increases asymptotically, the correct structure of the graph G (or any other I-equivalent structure) gets the maximum score.

The Bayesian score

Another class of scoring functions uses Bayesian principles to average out over both the space of possible structures as well as possible parameters to find the graph structure that best fits the data and the parameters. Scoring functions such as BDE and BDEU (variants of Bayesian Dirichlet) exist under the Bayesian umbrella, but they use different priors over structures and parameters.

As with all Bayesian approaches, the prior (both structure and parameters) will have a larger effect when the number of data instances is low. However, as the number of instances increases, the amount of data decreases the strength of the prior. Thus, for a low number of data instances, the Bayesian scores underfit the data.

The asymptotic behavior of Bayesian approaches begets scores that are similar to the BIC score, and they seldom overfit to the data.

In the following notebook (bnfinder.ipynb), we will now use the BNFinder library to learn the structure of a Bayesian network using score-based approaches.

The BNFinder tool has implementations of multiple score-based approaches such as BDE, MIT, and MDL. BNFinder can be installed using the `pip install BNFinder` command.

The BNFinder tool allows us to add prior information such as prospective parents and the known edges to the model prior to finding the relationships using a dataset.

Let's load the necessary imports and create the score function we will use (BDe). We will use the default parameter values, as shown in the following code:

```
fromBNfinder.BDEimportBDE
fromBNfinder.dataimportdataset

score=eval("BDE")(data_factor=1.0,chi_alpha=.9999,sloops=False)
score
```

The output of the preceding code is as follows:

`<BNfinder.BDE.BDE instance at 0x00000000124EB688>`

We created a dataset object and loaded it from a file. The `job_interview_samples.txt` file contains samples generated from the `libpgm'srandomsample()` method. The code that generated the samples can be found in the IPython Notebook `job_interview_samples.ipynb`.

Structure Learning

The dataset format that the `BNFinder` tool uses is the transpose of a normal dataset. If a normal dataset has three columns, each instance row contains three values. However, the `BNFinder` dataset format will have three rows, and one row will contain all the values for that column.

Let's create the following method that reads in a dataset, performs structure learning, and saves the output in a `.bif` format, as well as writes out the CPDs. The **Bayesian Interchange format (BIF)** is used by other tools that do Bayesian inference.

```
def learn_structure(sample_data,dataset_name):
    d = dataset(dataset_name).fromNewFile(open(sample_data))
    score2,g,subpars = d.learn(score=score,data_factor=1.0)
    d.write_bif(g,dataset_name+".bif")
    d.write_cpd(g,file(dataset_name+"_cpd.txt","w"))
    return score2,g,subpars
```

We'll now attempt to learn the structure from the sample data of the job interview network, as shown in the following code:

```
s,g,sp=learn_structure("job_interview_samples.txt","job_interview")
g
```

The graph information is as follows:

```
Admission(Admission) => Grades(-),
Experience(Experience) => Grades(+), Interview(+),
Grades(Grades) => Admission(-), Experience(+), Interview(+),
Interview(Interview) => Experience(+), Grades(+), Offer(+),
Offer(Offer) => Interview(+),
```

The output of the graph is a list of edges, with the parent on the left and the children on the right. The plus/minus signs indicate positive/negative correlations between nodes.

Although the code terminates quickly, it doesn't find the correct edges, with the exception of the edges between Interview-Offer and Grades-Admissions. The `BNFinder` tool does give the opportunity to add our intuitions/domain knowledge to the structure finding process by using the two methods: we can either define the known list of parents for a given vertex or specify a **regulator** (a technical term from the `BNFinder` tool's roots in biological network reconstruction), which will constrain the network to allow only listed nodes as root nodes or potential parents of all vertices.

We could add the regulator to the preamble section of the sample data file, which is saved in `job_interview_samples_preamble1.txt`. The following commands should work if you have the head command in your system shell.

The first line of the `preamble` section suggests that `Experience` and `Grades` are at the root of the network and have no parents, as shown in the following code:

!head -1 job_interview_samples_preamble1.txt

#regulators Experience Grades

```
s,g,sp=learn_structure("job_interview_samples_preamble1.txt","job_
interview")
g
```

The graph information is as follows:

```
Admission(Admission) =>
Experience(Experience) => Interview(+), Offer(+),
Grades(Grades) => Admission(-), Interview(+), Offer(+),
Interview(Interview) =>
Offer(Offer) =>
```

This time we see other kinds of errors, where the edge between `Interview` and `Offer` is gone. We add the following line to the `preamble` section (starting with the parents macro). This specifies that the parents for the `Interview` vertex are `Experience` and `Grades`, as shown in the following output:

!head -2 job_interview_samples_preamble2.txt

#regulators Experience Grades

#parents Interview Experience Grades

```
s,g,sp=learn_structure("job_interview_samples_preamble2.txt","job_
interview")
g
```

The graph information is as follows:

```
Admission(Admission) =>
Experience(Experience) => Interview(+), Offer(+),
Grades(Grades) => Admission(-), Interview(+), Offer(+),
Interview(Interview) =>
Offer(Offer) =>
```

Structure Learning

The edges obtained are missing an edge for Interview-Offer.

We can add three constraints, specifying the parents of `Experience` and `Offer` as well as the regulators. The code is as follows:

```
!head -3 job_interview_samples_preamble3.txt
#regulators Experience Grades
#parents Interview Experience Grades
#parents Offer Interview
```

```
s,g,sp=learn_structure("job_interview_samples_preamble3.txt","job_interview")
#save the file to open in cytoscape
net_str=g.to_SIF()
f=open("job_interview_sif.txt","w")
f.write(net_str)
f.close()
g
```

The graph information is as follows:

```
Admission(Admission) =>
Experience(Experience) => Interview(+),
Grades(Grades) => Admission(-), Interview(+),
Interview(Interview) => Offer(+),
Offer(Offer) =>
```

After specifying the preceding elements in the `preamble` section, we arrive at the correct network.

We can view the created network using the Cytoscape tool, which also allows us to export the nodes and edges found. The viewing and saving of the file in Cytoscape is done offline, and it is presented here. Cytoscape reads the `.sif` file created (in the preceding snippet) and can export a `.png` image, as shown in the following code:

```
Image("job_net.png")
```

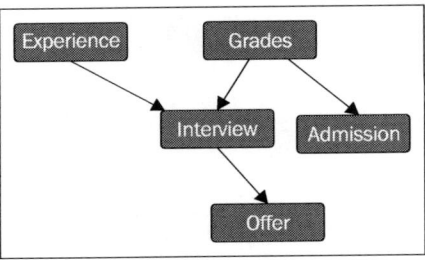

We can apply the `BNFinder` tool's score-based approach to larger datasets too. It is more efficient than the constraint-based approach in libpgm, but it needs handholding (by adding known edges) to prevent acyclicity and to complete quicker.

In the next snippet, we will attempt to learn the structure of a real-world network. This dataset consists of measurements of the states of a protein signaling network under different perturbations. While some of the signaling relationships are known prior to applying the structure learning algorithm, the learned structure is used to elucidate the traditionally reported relationships, as well as to infer novel network causalities, in the form of the Bayesian network.

The following example is taken from the `BNFinder` project documentation:

```
s,g,sp=learn_structure("sachs.inp","sachs")
net_str=g.to_SIF()
f=open("sachs_cpd.sif","w")
f.write(net_str)
f.close()
```

The following is the image generated by Cytoscape for the network. This network extracts 11 correct edges out of the 17 edges in the true dataset.

```
Image(filename='sachs_network.png')
```

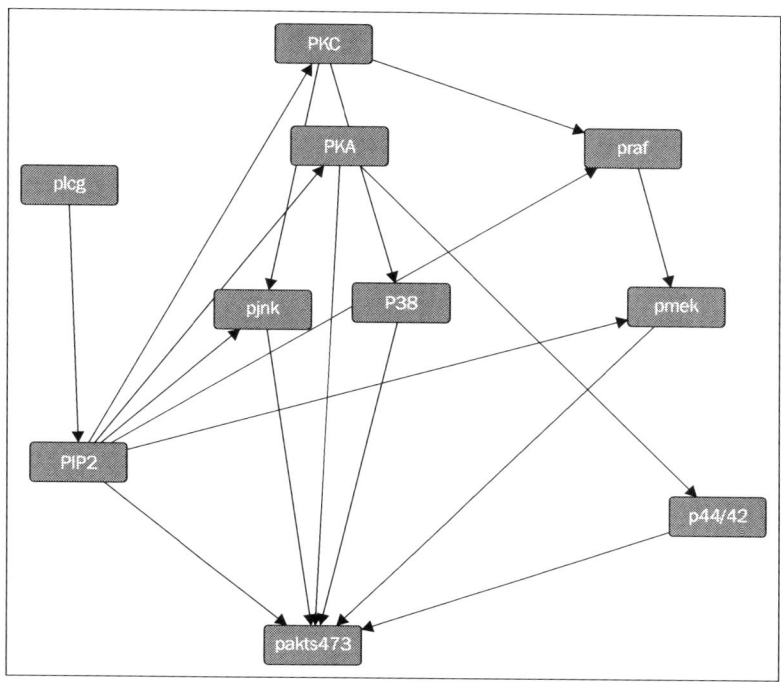

Structure Learning

We can conclude that it is not realistic to learn the perfect network structure from a dataset derived from a real-world network, especially if the number of random variables is greater than a small number. The structure learning algorithm is often employed by first incorporating the domain knowledge (the known edges between nodes) and then using the data to either empirically validate the plausibility of these edges or learn about new edges unknown to the domain experts.

Summary of score-based learning

From a computational perspective, the optimization perspective that the score-based approaches use are NP-hard, as compared to the constraint-based approaches that have low-polynomial time complexity. The other approaches gaining ground to avoid the NP hardness complexity are the heuristic search algorithms (such as greedy hill climbing, tabu search, and simulated annealing) to perform a local search of graph structures. These approaches use similar scoring functions to evaluate the structure's fit to data, and their efficiency is derived from the reduction of the space of graph structures to search in.

Since we use often use the learned structure to run inference queries, we must recall that inference in Bayesian networks is NP-hard. Even approximate inference is NP-hard. Therefore, we strive to learn graph structures that will allow us to get quick inference. The PGM community has therefore gravitated to learning specific classes of structure (such as trees and forests) for which both structure learning and inference is a bit more manageable.

Trees have been preferred due to their desirable features. Their structure can be learned using optimization approaches even in high dimensions, and the number of parameters can be kept low.

Summary

In this chapter, we had a first look at learning the structure of a network from data. We looked at two approaches, one based on constraints and another based on scoring functions. Also, we ran some Python samples to see these algorithms in action. We learned that to find the best structure, we have to search over an exponentially large number of structures, and therefore trees and forests are preferred structures over general graphs.

In the next chapter, we will learn about parameter learning and how to define the parameters for graph structures that we already know.

Parameter Learning

In this chapter, we will learn about the methods to estimate the parameters of a PGM. We start with toy examples such as estimating the bias in a coin flipping experiment.

Our journey, so far, on the PGM trail can be compared to the task of a sales person (let's call him Jake) trying to sell a software package to a large scale company. He may attempt to identify the different people involved, such as the end users of the software, managers, and the procurement department, among others. This is akin to finding random variables (including latent or hidden random variables) in a graphical model. Jake will try to make connections with people who could be interested or by identifying, for example, who influences whom, who are the decision makers, and what is the organizational hierarchy. This is similar to making connections between random variables in a graphical model, something we explored in the previous chapter.

Also important to Jake is the degree of influence between people, considering some people exert a greater degree of influence than others. He finds out that the purchasing decision is made by Bob, and that Alice and Charlie have a personal connection with Bob, but Bob trusts Alice's opinion far more than Charlie's (in other words, Alice's degree of influence on Bob is greater than that of Charlie). Thus, Jake has a higher chance of a sale if he provides Alice with a demo of the software he is selling, as opposed to Charlie.

This task of determining the degree of influence between the connections is called parameter learning, which we will discuss later in the chapter. Parameter learning is required for both directed (Bayesian) and undirected (Markov) networks.

Parameter Learning

The parameter learning landscape we will explore consists of two broad areas. The first is called **maximum likelihood estimates** (**MLEs**). Despite the complicated sounding name, MLEs are often easy to calculate by taking counts of event occurrences (depending on the type of distribution). The second approach uses Bayesian statistics. The choice of approach is debatable (and many references can be found online for `Bayesian` versus `Frequentist`) and each approach has its pros and cons.

We start with a toy example. We toss a thumbtack a number of times to learn the probability of it landing on its head using the Bayesian and MLE approaches. The following image shows a thumbtack:

The tosses of the thumbtack can be modeled using the Bernoulli distribution, which is a probability distribution that takes the values of 1 (heads) with probability θ and 0 (tails) with probability $1-\theta$, where θ is the bias of the thumbtack.

If we toss the thumbtack 100 times and record the results, we get a sequence of 100 events similar to *{H,H,T,H,H....}*. This sequence of results is referred to as **independent and identically distributed** (**i.i.d.**) samples that are drawn from the same distribution and independent of each other.

The Bayesian network for the thumbtack flips is seen in the following diagram. (It is similar to the Naive Bayesian network in *Chapter 2, Directed Graphical Models*).

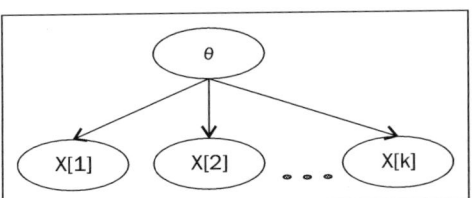

We expect that, with a sufficiently large number of flips, we get close to the true estimate of the bias. Let's consider the case of the following results: {H, T, H, T}. The probability of the first heads is theta, $P(H) = \theta$, and that of the second tails is $P(T|H)$. Since the tosses are independent, $P(T) = (1-\theta)$.

Therefore, the probability of achieving the sequence {H, T, H, T}, which contains two heads and two tails, is $\theta^2(1-\theta)^2$. We can generalize further and state that a sequence containing heads (h) and tails (t) will have a probability equal to $\theta^h(1-\theta)^t$.

The likelihood function

In probability, we start with a known parameter and predict the data. The concept of likelihood is starting with the data and predicting the parameter. The maximum likelihood is the value of the parameter that maximizes the possibility of the data, or in other words, maximizes the value of the likelihood function.

The value of the maximum likelihood in the case of the Bernoulli distribution is as follows:

$$\hat{\theta} = \frac{number\ of\ heads}{number\ of\ heads + number\ of\ tails}$$

We see that the ordering of the sequence has no effect, and all we need are the counts of the number of heads and tails.

There is one shortcoming to the MLE approach: the parameter estimate does not indicate our confidence in the parameter. The value for theta can be 0.7, regardless of the number of flips (7 heads from 10 flips or 7000 heads from 10000 flips). It is clear that we have more confidence when the result is obtained from 10000 flips as opposed to 10; however, MLE does not give us that picture.

The number of heads and tails from the thumbtack (Bernoulli) experiment is called sufficient statistics. This is because to get the maximum likelihood estimate, we only need the number (of heads and tails) and not the sequence. Different types of distributions require different sufficient statistics. For example, for a multinomial distribution (such as throwing a six-sided dice), sufficient statistics are the count of times the result is one of these values: {1, 2, 3, 4, 5, 6}.

Parameter Learning

Parameter learning example using MLE

In the `Chap5_thumbtack_mle.ipynb` IPython Notebook, we will examine the parameters of a thumbtack using maximum likelihood estimation.

We first import the `bernoulli` distribution. Working backwards, we set the bias of the thumbtack (by choosing a value for the parameter θ) and then flip the thumbtack a number of times (by sampling random values), as shown in the following code:

```
from scipy.stats import bernoulli
import numpy as np
import matplotlib.pyplot as plt
import matplotlib

param_theta=0.3
num_flips=100
```

To generate the flips of the thumbtack, we simply call the `rvs` function (random variates) on the `bernoulli` object. To generate 10 flips, we run the following code:

```
bernoulli.rvs(0.3,size=10)
```

The output of the preceding code is as follows:

array([0, 1, 0, 0, 1, 1, 1, 1, 1, 0])

The sufficient statistics required to estimate the parameters are simply the counts of the heads and tails. Let's write a function that generates some flips, counts the number of heads, and gives us an estimate of the parameter θ, by dividing the number of heads by the total number of flips.

The following function returns a tuple. The first is the cumulative estimate and the second is the final estimate.

```
def estimate_param(param, num_flips):
    res=bernoulli.rvs(param,size=num_flips)

    r_est=[np.sum(res[:i])/float(i) for i in range(1,len(res)+1)]

    final_estimate=ones/float(num_flips)

    return r_est,final_estimate

print estimate_param(param_theta,num_flips=10)
```

The output of the preceding code is as follows:

```
([0.0, 0.0, 0.0, 0.0, 0.2, 0.16, 0.14, 0.125, 0.11, 0.1], 0.1)
```

The actual value you see when this is executed can be quite different due to the random nature of the flipping process. The following code determines the bias for an ever increasing number of samples. The generated plot shows that as the number of samples increase, the estimate is closer to the true value (0.3), as described by the horizontal line. Each of the individual subplots shows that the estimate improves as the number of samples increases.

```
x=[10,100,1000]

colors = matplotlib.rcParams['axes.color_cycle']

f, axarr = plt.subplots(len(x), 1)
f.tight_layout()
plt.subplots_adjust(hspace = 1)

for i, samples in enumerate(x):
    est,res=estimate_param(param_theta,samples)
    ax1 = plt.subplot(len(x),1,i+1)
    ax1.plot(range(samples),est , label=samples, alpha=0.4, lw=3)
    msg="number of samples ",samples
    
    ax1.set_title(msg)
    ax1.set_xlabel("$x$")
    
    ax1.set_ylim([0,0.8])
    ax1.axhline(y=res, xmin=0, xmax=1,linewidth=1, color='r')
    ax1.axhline(y=param_theta, xmin=0, xmax=1,linewidth=1, color='b')

plt.show()
```

Parameter Learning

The output of the preceding code is as follows:

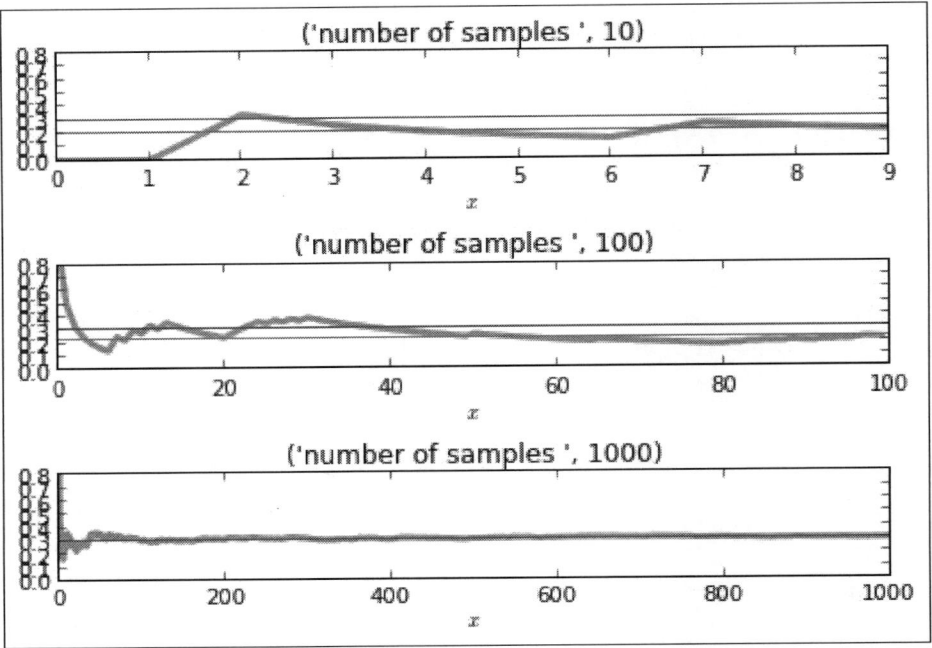

MLE for Bayesian networks

Now that we have seen how to estimate using MLE, we will try to apply the same in a Bayesian network. We have seen how the structure of the Bayesian network allows us to decompose a large joint distribution into a smaller set of CPDs, and the same decomposability comes to our rescue during parameter estimation.

Let's take the example of a small Bayesian network with two binary random variables, X and Y, which are connected thus $X \rightarrow Y$. This network has two CPDs that are parameterized by θ^x (for X0 and X1) and $\theta^{y|x}$ (for the four entries in the CPD for Y given X). The dataset we are provided with is a set of instances of the form $<X^a, Y^b>$.

Our goal (in MLE) is to find the (set of) parameters θ that maximize the likelihood of the data.

It turns out that the likelihood function $L(\theta:D)$ (that is, the likelihood of parameter θ given D) decomposes into a set of two terms, one for each random variable X and Y. Each term is called the local likelihood function, which measures how it can be predicted given its parents.

For the random variable X, similar to what we have seen from the earlier section, the values of parameters are as follows:

$$\theta^{x^0} = \frac{M[x^0]}{M[x^0] + M[x^1]} \text{ and } \theta^{x^1} = \frac{M[x^1]}{M[x^0] + M[x^1]}.$$

Where M is the sufficient statistics, for example, $M[x^0]$ is the number of times we have seen x^0.

Similarly, the values of the four parameters of $\theta^{y|x}$ are acquired by taking similar counts. The specific value of $\theta^{y^1|x^0}$ is as follows:

$$\theta^{y^1|x^0} = \frac{M[x^0, y^1]}{M[x^0, y^1] + M[x^0, y^0]} = \frac{M[x^0, y^1]}{M[x^0]}$$

Here $M[x^0, y^1]$ is the number of times we see x^0, y^1 in the dataset and $M[x^0]$ is the number of times we see x^0, regardless of the value of Y.

For larger networks, the MLE parameter estimates are obtained by independently estimating the parameters for each CPD using the local likelihood function. These can then be combined to form the MLE solution for the whole network.

For each random variable X with parents U, the MLE parameter is $\theta^{x|u} = \frac{M[x,u]}{M[u]}$, where $M[u] = \sum_x M[u,x]$.

Bayesian parameter learning example using MLE

In the `job_interview_libpgm.ipynb` IPython Notebook, we will use the libpgm implementation of maximum likelihood estimates to learn the parameters of the CPDs in the job interview network.

Here is the code from `libpgm` that loads the CPDs, as shown before:

```
from libpgm.graphskeleton import GraphSkeleton
from libpgm.nodedata import NodeData
from libpgm.discretebayesiannetwork import DiscreteBayesianNetwork
from libpgm.tablecpdfactor import TableCPDFactor
from libpgm.pgmlearner import PGMLearner
import pandas as pd
```

Parameter Learning

```
nd = NodeData()
skel = GraphSkeleton()
jsonpath="job_interview.txt"
nd.load(jsonpath)
skel.load(jsonpath)
skel.toporder()
```

We can create the Bayesian network and get random samples using the following code:

```
bn = DiscreteBayesianNetwork(skel, nd)
samples=bn.randomsample(2000)
```

In the following code, we instantiate the PGMLearner class. The discrete_mle_estimateparams method already knows the structure of the network. As discussed in the earlier section, the estimates for each CPD only needs information from the parents, and this decomposition makes it possible to learn the parameters of each CPD:

```
learner = PGMLearner()
result = learner.discrete_mle_estimateparams(skel, samples)
```

The following are the results for the CPD from the samples for the Interview node. The leftmost column consisting of the values 0 and 1 are those from the parent's assignments ([0,0]) indicates Experience = 0 and Grades = 0), and the columns with headings 0, 1, and 2 indicate probabilities for the Interview node taking the values of 0, 1, and 2.

```
pd.DataFrame(result.Vdata['Interview']['cprob']).transpose()
```

The output of the preceding code is as follows:

	0	1	2
['0', '0']	0.809582	0.165848	0.024570
['0', '1']	0.321678	0.396853	0.281469
['1', '0']	0.323204	0.591160	0.085635
['1', '1']	0.115079	0.182540	0.702381

The following result is the CPD parameters from the original network. Some values in the result are a reasonably close approximation to each other, while other values have errors in the range of 20 percent.

```
pd.DataFrame(bn.Vdata['Interview']['cprob']).transpose()
```

The output of the preceding code is as follows:

	0	1	2
['0', '0']	0.8	0.18	0.02
['0', '1']	0.3	0.60	0.10
['1', '0']	0.3	0.40	0.30
['1', '1']	0.1	0.20	0.70

Data fragmentation

For a network with a large number of random variables, with each random variable taking on a large number of values, we see that the number of data instances for each unique assignment to the parent and child variables becomes vanishingly small. In some cases, we have no instances at all. Therefore, the parameters estimated from a few data instances available, usually overfit the data or return the value zero where there are no instances available.

Therefore, as the dimensionality of the parent set increases, it becomes progressively harder to reliably estimate the parameters. This becomes a limiting factor in our ability to learn Bayesian networks from data.

Effects of data fragmentation on parameter estimation

In this following `data_segmentation.ipynb` IPython Notebook, we will see the effect of data segmentation on parameter estimation using maximum likelihood. We have a small network defined in `small_network.txt`, which has two random variables, $X \rightarrow Y$, connected by an arc. The parent X takes five values and the child Y takes two.

We first load the network from the file and create a `DiscreteBayesianNetwork` file as shown in the following code:

```
from libpgm.graphskeleton import GraphSkeleton
from libpgm.nodedata import NodeData
from libpgm.discretebayesiannetwork import DiscreteBayesianNetwork
from libpgm.pgmlearner import PGMLearner

nd = NodeData()
skel = GraphSkeleton()
jsonpath="small_network.txt"
nd.load(jsonpath)
```

Parameter Learning

```
skel.load(jsonpath)
skel.toporder()

bn = DiscreteBayesianNetwork(skel, nd)
```

In the following code, we will create a function that learns the parameters of the network with data sampled from it. We print the estimated parameter value of the assignment X = 3 and Y = 0 after drawing 50 samples. We run the same function a few times to compare the results we get. Since sampling is random, you can get different results when you run the following:

```
def learn_param(num_samp=50):
    data = bn.randomsample(num_samp)
    # instantiate learner
    learner = PGMLearner()

    # estimate parameters from data and skeleton
    result = learner.discrete_mle_estimateparams(skel, data)
    numer=len([1 for m in data if m["X"]=='3' and m["Y"]=='0'])
    denom=len([1 for m in data if m["X"]=='3'])

    print "numerator:",numer," denominator:",denom," result=",numer/float(denom)

[learn_param() for _ in range(5)]
```

The output of the preceding code is as follows:

```
numerator: 1   denominator: 6    result= 0.166666666667
numerator: 2   denominator: 6    result= 0.333333333333
numerator: 2   denominator: 10   result= 0.2
numerator: 1   denominator: 4    result= 0.25
numerator: 2   denominator: 12   result= 0.166666666667
```

We see that the result varies a lot because the number of interesting samples (X == 3 and Y == 0) is low in the sampled dataset. The actual value that we've set in the file is 0.2.

```
nd.Vdata["Y"]["cprob"]["['3']"][0]
```

The following is the output of the preceding code:

```
0.2
```

It is only when we increase the number of samples that we get the values that are close, as shown in the following code:

```
[learn_param(5000) for _ in range(3)]
```

The following is the output of the preceding code:

numerator: 160   denominator: 720   result= 0.222222222222
numerator: 156   denominator: 763   result= 0.204456094364
numerator: 156   denominator: 757   result= 0.20607661823

Although it is a small network with a single parent, the parent takes on an increasing number of discrete values and we get poor maximum likelihood estimates. Data fragmentation can be avoided by modeling networks as follows:

- Restricting the number of parents for a given node
- Restricting the number of discrete values for the parent nodes, wherever possible

Bayesian parameter estimation

In the MLE example, the data alone was used to estimate the parameter under observation. However, in many situations, we have a fairly good idea about the parameter being observed. If we were asked about the fairness of a coin, we are often fairly certain that the value of the parameter is 0.5, that is, heads and tails are equally likely. Bayesian statistics allows us to take this prior intuition into account and find a posterior that is informed by both the prior as well as the data. Even though we think the coin is fair, if we get 30,000 heads out of 100,000 flips, we will be convinced that the parameter is close to 0.3 and not 0.5, as surmised earlier.

We start the analysis by reversing our assumptions that each flip is independent and θ is a fixed quantity. We assume that θ is a random variable and each successive flip tells us more about the value of θ. We assume that the flips are conditionally independent given θ.

The joint distribution of the tosses and θ is as follows:

$$P(x[1],\ldots x[k],\theta) = P(\theta)P(x[1],\ldots x[k]|\theta)$$

Assuming conditional independence between tosses, ensuing is the right-hand term:

$$= P(\theta)\prod_{i=1}^{k} P(x[i]|\theta) = P(\theta)\theta^{H}(1-\theta)^{T}$$

Here H and T are the number of heads and tails, respectively.

We can use this joint distribution to specify the posterior over θ, as shown in the formula:

$$= P(\theta \mid x[1],\ldots x[k]) = \frac{P(\theta) P(x[1],\ldots x[k] \mid \theta)}{P(x[1],\ldots x[k])}$$

The first two terms in the numerator are the prior and likelihood, while the denominator is a normalizing constant that makes the right-hand side a proper density function.

The Bayesian methods, of course, allow us to use informative priors (unlike say, the uniform prior) in cases where we have a strong intuition about the probability distribution.

An example of Bayesian methods for parameter learning

In the `thumbtack_Bayesian.ipynb` IPython Notebook, we will use the Bayesian methods to determine the bias of the thumbtack, obtained from parameter θ.

We will use the excellent PyMC library for the same. Please install PyMC using `easy_install PyMC`.

We shall avoid going into the finer details of PyMC at the moment. Excellent documentation for PyMC can be found both in the PyMC docs as well as in the book, *Probabilistic Programming and Bayesian Methods for Hackers, Cam Davidson-Pilon*, available at `http://camdavidsonpilon.github.io/Probabilistic-Programming-and-Bayesian-Methods-for-Hackers/`.

For estimating theta, we will first generate 30 samples from the Bernoulli distribution, where the controlling parameter takes the value of `0.3` (which corresponds to roughly 30 percent of the generated values of 1, and the rest being 0).

We attempt to find the parameters of the posterior distribution, and learned that the posterior depends on the prior as well as the data. There are many choices of prior available to us. In this case, we will use the uniform prior. Since we have little idea about the bias of the thumbtack, we believe it can lie anywhere between 0 and 1.

The PyMC model contains two variables. The first is a uniform prior, which represents our belief that the value of the parameter can be anywhere between 0 and 1. The second is the Bernoulli variable, to which we provide data.

The two variables are linked in a parent-child relationship; the uniform prior is the designated parent of the Bernoulli variable.

We use the following types of PyMC variables:

- **Stochastic**: This is the `uni_prior` variable that can take different values based on the parameter theta
- **Deterministic**: This is the `bern` variable, whose values are decided by its parents

Finally, all the variables in the model are wrapped in a `model` object.

For all the variables whose values are not `true`, PyMC's simulations will marginally affect the variable's value during the simulation. The value (of the `uni_prior` variable in our case) will start to approximate its posterior values, as shown in the following code:

```
from pymc import *
from scipy.stats import bernoulli
import matplotlib.pyplot as plt
import pymc.Matplot as plott


def create_model(data):
    #create a uniform prior, the lower and upper limits of which are 0 and 1
    uni_prior = Uniform('uni_prior', lower=0,upper=1.0 )
    bern = Bernoulli('bern',p=uni_prior, value=data,observed=True)
    model=Model([uni_prior,bern])
    return model
```

Samples drawn from the prior distribution show that the prior is uniformly distributed between 0 and 1 on the *x* axis, as shown in the following code:

```
uni_prior = Uniform('uni_prior', lower=0,upper=1.0 )

samples = [uni_prior.random() for i in range(20000)]
plt.hist(samples, bins=100, normed=True )
plt.title("Prior distribution for $\ theta$")
plt.show()
```

Parameter Learning

The output of the preceding code is as follows:

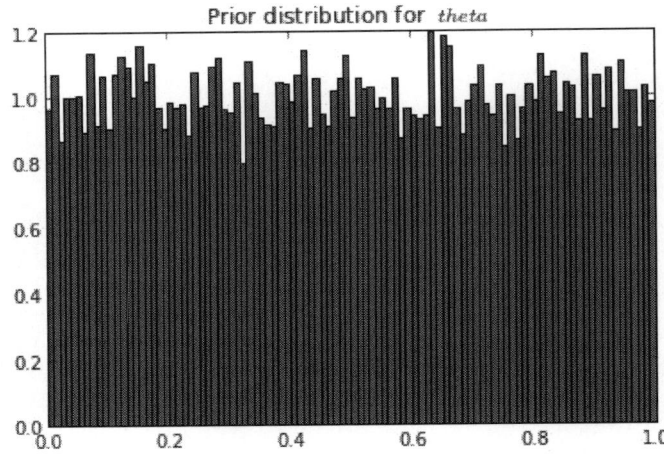

In the following snippet, we use the sampling method **Markov Chain Monte Carlo** (**MCMC**). MCMC is a method used to draw samples from the posterior distribution. We draw 5000 samples and a histogram of the samples (called traces in MCMC parlance). In Bayesian statistics, the parameter theta is represented as a random variable and not a single value.

```
sample_size=30

def get_traces(sample_size):
    data=bernoulli.rvs(0.3,size=sample_size)
    model=create_model(data)
    model.seed()
    mc1 = MCMC(model)
    mc1.sample(iter=5000,burn=1000)
    return mc1,mc1.trace('uni_prior')[:]

mc1,traces=get_traces(sample_size)
plott.histogram(traces,"uni_prior")
```

The output of the preceding code is as follows:

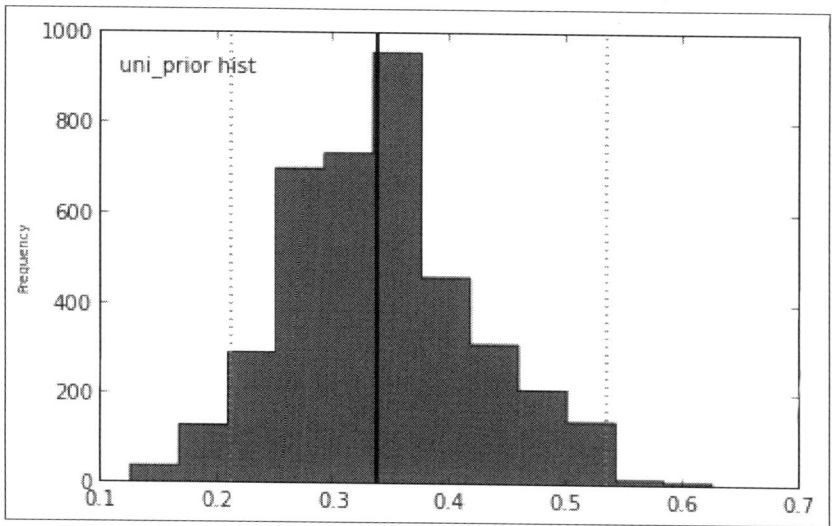

We plot the posterior distribution of the parameter theta. Note that the distribution has quite a bit of variance, and the peak of the distribution (indicated by a black vertical line) does not correspond to 0.3, which is the true value of the parameter theta. The peak of the distribution hill is called a point estimate in Bayesian parlance, which is analogous to the best estimate if we want to represent the parameter theta as a single value.

In the following code snippet, we plot the posterior distribution for an increasing number of samples. We used only 30 samples for the initial model. Can increasing the number of samples help improve the estimate for the parameter?

```
num_samples=[20,50,100,500,5000]
for i in num_samples:
    m,traces=get_traces(i)
    plott.histogram(traces,"num samples = "+str(i),datarange=(0,0.6))
```

Parameter Learning

The output of the preceding code is as follows:

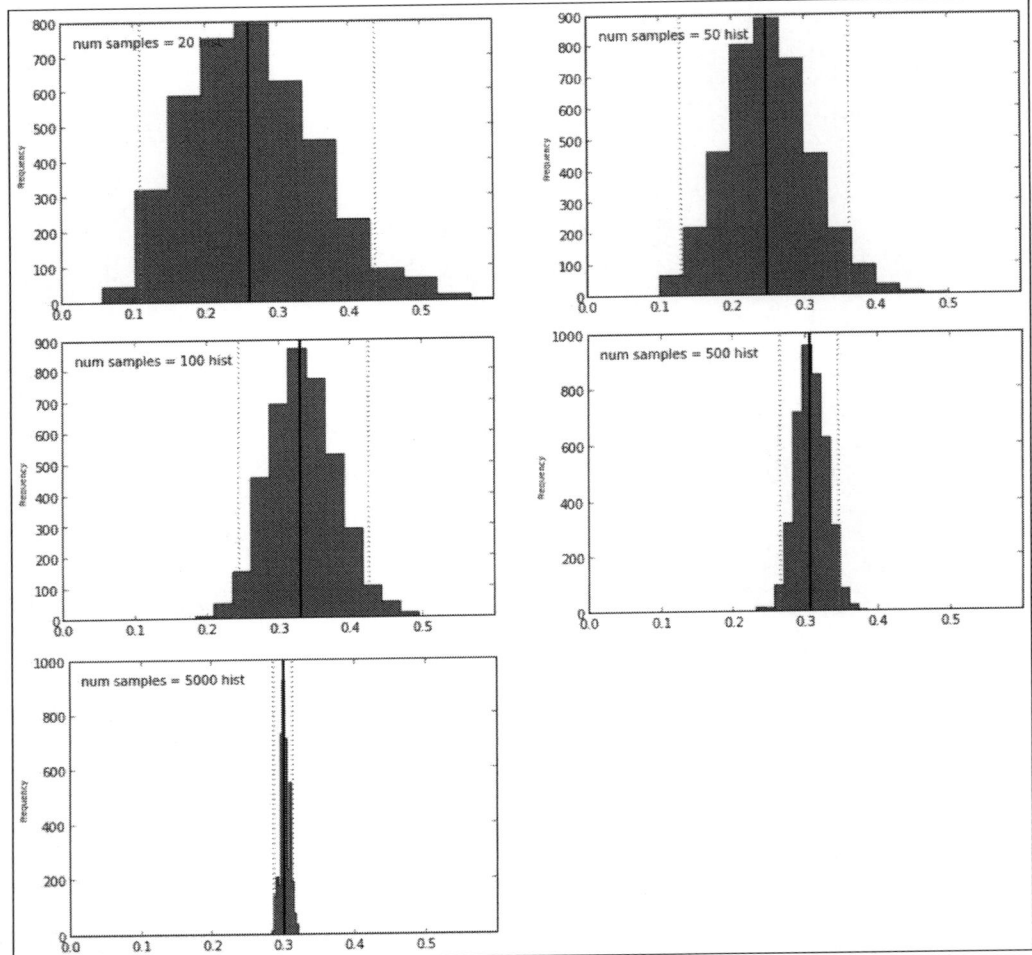

We see that an increasing number of samples makes the distribution hill sharper, which indicates its growing confidence in its estimate of the parameter theta.

We use PyMC's graphing capabilities to create an image of the hierarchical model. We also need to install a few python libraries such as pydot and pygraphviz (and install base graphviz as well).

We create the dot format graph representation using this simple one-line code:

```
gdot=pymc.graph.dag(mc1)
```

Viewing the file is also quite simple. We just write the dot object to a .png file and view it as shown in the following code:

```
from IPython.display import Image
gdot.write_png('thumbtack_graph.png')
Image(filename='thumbtack_graph.png')
```

The output of the preceding code is as follows:

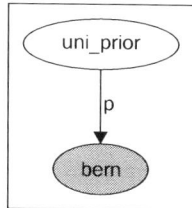

Bayesian estimation for the Bayesian network

Similar to the Bayesian case for the estimation of a single parameter, using the Bayesian framework requires us to specify the joint distribution for all the data instances and unknown parameters.

For the parameters we are trying to estimate, if we decide to have the parameters priori independent (which may not be applicable in all cases), then calculating the posterior becomes easier (which is analogous to likelihood decomposition in MLE). If we have a network comprising two nodes ($X \to Y$), then we can calculate the posterior of θ^x independently of the posterior over $\theta^{y|x}$, and the same decomposability can be generalized to larger networks.

Example of Bayesian estimation

In the `learn_cpd_Bayesian.ipynb` IPython Notebook, we'll use PyMC to estimate the parameters of one CPD from the job interview network, as shown in the following code:

```
from libpgm.graphskeleton import GraphSkeleton
from libpgm.nodedata import NodeData
from libpgm.discretebayesiannetwork import DiscreteBayesianNetwork
import pandas as pd

from pymc import *
```

Parameter Learning

```
import matplotlib.pyplot as plt
from pymc.Matplot import plot

nd = NodeData()
skel = GraphSkeleton()
jsonpath="job_interview.txt"
nd.load(jsonpath)
skel.load(jsonpath)
skel.toporder()
bn = DiscreteBayesianNetwork(skel, nd)
```

The CPD that we are trying to learn is the `Interview` CPD, as shown in the following code:

```
pd.DataFrame(bn.Vdata['Interview']['cprob']).transpose()
```

The output for the preceding code is as follows:

	0	1	2
['0', '0']	0.8	0.18	0.02
['0', '1']	0.3	0.60	0.10
['1', '0']	0.3	0.40	0.30
['1', '1']	0.1	0.20	0.70

The CPD has 12 unique probabilities. Each row in the preceding output corresponds to one particular assignment to its parents (`Experience` and `Grades`) and can be represented by a multinomial distribution. In this particular case, `Interview` takes three values, and therefore the multinomial representing each row can be likened to a three-sided dice.

Since there are four unique assignments of the parent variables, we'll need to learn the parameters for four `Multinomial` variables.

Finally, we run MCMC sampling on this model and observe the posterior as follows:

```
def create_model(data,num_draws):
    partial_dirich = pymc.Dirichlet(name="partial_dirich",theta=[1.0, 1.0, 1.0])
    full_dirich=pymc.CompletedDirichlet(name="full_dirich",D=partial_dirich)
    multi = pymc.Multinomial(
            name="multi",
            value=data,
            n=num_draws,
            p=full_dirich,
            observed=True)
```

```
    model=Model([partial_dirich,full_dirich,multi])
    return model

def run_mcmc(model,**kwargs):
    mcmc = pymc.MCMC(model)
    mcmc.sample(**kwargs)
    return mcmc
```

The preceding snippet contains a PyMC model, consisting of the following three variables in a tree:

- `Dirichlet`: The prior is represented by this distribution, which allows us an initial prior comprising a set of three probability values that sum up to 1. In PyMC, the `Dirichlet` stochastic variable only stores $k - 1$ probabilities (for a multinomial with k outcomes) because the kth value can be calculated since the probabilities sum to 1.
- `CompletedDirichlet`: For simplicity, we define it as a child of the `Dirichlet` variable, and this makes it easier to represent all the k values (k = 3 in this case).
- `Multinomial`: This is the last variable and is a child of the `CompletedDirichlet` object. We will sample data from the job interview network and pass it to the `Multinomial` variable.

Note that in the thumbtack estimation problem, we learned the estimate of just one Bernoulli distribution. In this case, we have to learn the parameter estimates of four separate multinomial distributions.

Therefore, we sample the job interview network four times, once with each assignment to its parents. We'll start with the first parent assignment: { *Experience* = 0, *Grades* = 0}, which helps us learn the parameters of the first row of the CPD.

The samples that can be consumed by PyMC need a specific format, consisting of the results of a series of experiments.

Let's first understand the term experiment. In the single run of an experiment, sampling from the network is done *n* times (similar to *n* throws of the three-sided dice). This will give us a sequence of 0s, 1s, and 2s of length *n*. We prune this sequence to get the frequencies of occurrence of 0, 1, and 2 (performed in the `get_counts` method), as shown in the following code:

```
def get_counts(vals):
    b = {0:0,1:0,2:0}
    for item in vals:
        b[item] = b.get(item, 0) + 1
```

Parameter Learning

```
        return np.array(b.values())
get_counts([0,1,2,0,1])
```

The output of the preceding code is as follows:

array([2, 2, 1])

The resulting array tells us that 0 and 1 appeared twice and 2 appeared once.

We perform several such experiments (10 in this specific case), collate the frequencies, and pass this as data to the Multinomial variable in our PyMC model.

We then run MCMC sampling on the PyMC model, and as during a random walk, the value in the full_dirich variable in the PyMC model starts to approximate the true multinomial distribution, as shown in the following code:

```
def get_relevant_samples(experiments,evidence,num_samples=10):
    ''' for n experiments, sample and add the frequencies obtained.'''
    res=[]
    for i in xrange(experiments):
        vals=[float(i['Interview']) for i in bn.randomsample(num_samples,evidence)]
        res.append(get_counts(vals))
    return res

def plot_traces(traces):
    colors = ["#348ABD", "#A60628","#884732"]

    plt.plot(np.arange(len(traces)), traces[:,:, 0], c=colors[0])
    plt.plot(np.arange(len(traces)), traces[:,:, 1], c=colors[1])
    plt.plot(np.arange(len(traces)), traces[:,:, 2], c=colors[2])
    plt.title("traces of posterior ")
    plt.show()

def estimate_parameters(evidence,**kwargs):
    ''' run a few experiments, get the data, and estimate the parameter '''
    experiments=10
    samples=get_relevant_samples(experiments,evidence,num_samples=10)
    model=create_model(samples,experiments)
    mc=run_mcmc(model,**kwargs)

    traces=mc.trace('full_dirich')[:]
    return [np.mean(traces[:, :,0]),np.mean(traces[:,:, 1]),np.mean(traces[:,:, 2])],traces
```

We first determine the parameters for the parent assignment, *{Experience = 0, Grades = 0}*, as shown in the following code, and plot the traces. We see three separate plot lines. These are the values for the three probabilities in the multinomial distribution, which should sum up to 1.

```
means,traces=estimate_parameters(dict(Grades='0',Experience='0'),iter=5000)
plot_traces(traces)
```

The output of the preceding code is as follows:

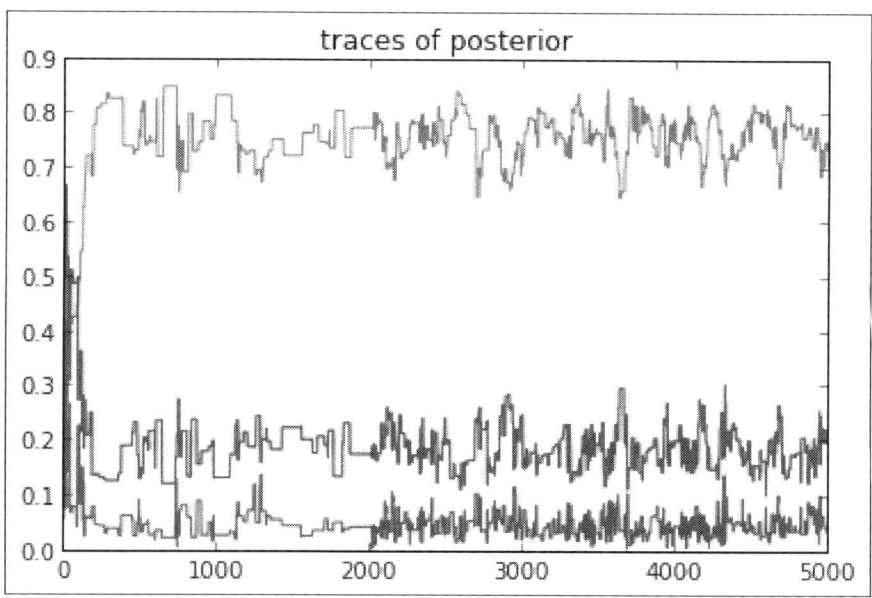

In the preceding plot, we take the first 5000 traces. We see that the posterior moves around initially and then settles down a bit. If we add a `burn` parameter to PyMC prior to the sampling, the algorithm discards the first *n* samples specified by the `burn` value and collects the next traces. Since the MCMC algorithm takes time doing a random walk starting from the prior, specifying a `burn` value allows the algorithm to discard traces that are ostensibly not from the true posterior distribution, as shown in the following code:

```
means,traces=estimate_parameters(dict(Grades='0',Experience='0'),iter=20000,burn=1000)
plot_traces(traces)
```

Parameter Learning

The output of the preceding code is as follows:

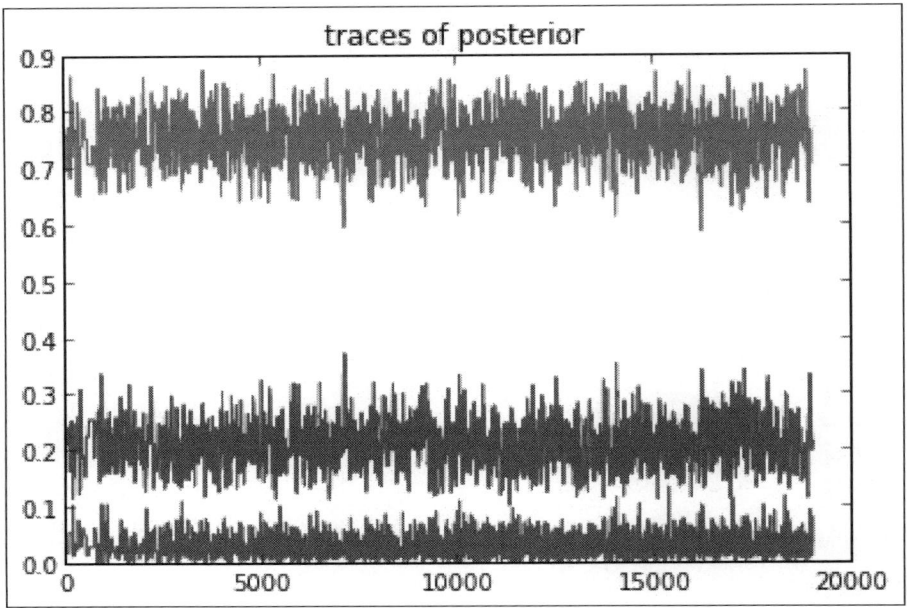

We see that the individual probabilities have converged. We first determined the parameters for the parent assignment {Experience = 0, Grades = 0}. To learn the values for all the joint assignments to the parent variable, we run the following snippet:

```
all_parent_assignments=[['0','0'],['0','1'],['1','0'],['1','1']]
res=[]
for i,j in all_parent_assignments:
    evidence=dict(Grades=i,Experience=j)
    means,traces=estimate_parameters(evidence,iter=50000,burn=10000)
    res.append([[i,j]]+means)

pd.DataFrame(res,columns=['parent_assignment',0,1,2])
```

The output of the preceding code is as follows:

	par_assign	0	1	2
0	[0, 0]	0.835853	0.144636	0.019511
1	[0, 1]	0.303323	0.464297	0.232380
2	[1, 0]	0.291015	0.563842	0.145143
3	[1, 1]	0.126254	0.223568	0.650178

We compare the preceding posterior means with the true probabilities specified in the following job interview network. Some of the learned values are very close to the true values, while others differ from the ground truth by as much as 16 percent.

```
pd.DataFrame(bn.Vdata['Interview']['cprob']).transpose()
```

The output of the preceding code is as follows:

```
par_assign      0       1       2
['0', '0']      0.8     0.18    0.02
['0', '1']      0.3     0.60    0.10
['1', '0']      0.3     0.40    0.30
['1', '1']      0.1     0.20    0.70
```

Summary

In this chapter, we have learned about the parameter estimation problem. We first estimated the parameters of a thumbtack using two approaches, MLE and Bayesian. We then extended those foundations to determine the parameters of a Bayesian network using MLE.

Having walked through the basics of the structure and parameter learning, in the next set of chapters, we will use networks to answer our queries using various types of inference approaches.

6
Exact Inference Using Graphical Models

So far we have learned about the methods to build graphical models. In this chapter, we shall employ over fully specified graphical models to various inference engines to obtain answers to the questions.

Before we start on the inference trail, we shall learn about the complexity of the inference problem. Using different types of inference is appropriate in certain contexts, and we will learn which type is applicable where, and then experiment with both approaches.

Complexity of inference

A graphical model can be used to answer both probability queries and MAP queries. The most straightforward way to use this model is to generate the joint distribution and sum out all the variables, except the ones we are interested in. However, we need to determine and specify the joint distribution where an exponential blowup happens.

In worst-case scenarios, we need to determine the exact inference in NP-hard. By the word exact, we mean specifying the probability values with a certain precision (say, five digits after the decimals). Suppose we tone down our precision requirements (for example, only up to two digits after the decimals). Now, is the (approximate) inference task any easier? Unfortunately not—even approximate inference is NP-hard, that is, getting values is far better than random guessing (50 percent or a probability of 0.5), which takes exponential time.

It might seem like inference is a hopeless task, but that is only in the worst case. In general cases, we can use exact inference to solve certain classes of real-world problems (such as Bayesian networks that have a small number of discrete random variables). Of course, for larger problems, we have to resort to approximate inference.

Since this book is about graphical models in Python, let's digress into the choice of tools we can use to run inference.

Real-world issues

Since inference is a task that is NP-hard, inference engines are written in languages that are as close to bare metal as possible; usually in C or C++. Since this is a book about PGMs in Python, we have a few choices to make:

- Use Python implementations of inference algorithms. Complete and mature packages for these are uncommon.
- Use inference engines that have a Python interface, such as Stan (mc-stan.org). This choice serves a good balance between running the Python code and a fast inference implementation.
- Use inference engines that do not have a Python interface, which is true for majority of the inference engines out there. A fairly comprehensive list can be found at http://en.wikipedia.org/wiki/Bayesian_network#Software. The use of Python here is limited to creating a file that describes the model in a format that the inference engine can consume.

In the chapters on inference, we will stick to the first two choices in the list. We will use native Python implementations (of inference algorithms) to peek into the interiors of the inference algorithms while running toy-sized problems, and then use an external inference engine with Python interfaces to try out a more real-world problem.

Using the Variable Elimination algorithm

In this section, we shall learn the Variable Elimination algorithm. In the VarElim_asia.ipynb IPython Notebook, we shall use the Asia network to understand the details of this algorithm.

The Asia network (http://www.bnlearn.com/bnrepository/#asia) is a toy Bayesian network used for patient diagnosis. The network tries to elicit the possibility of lung cancer or tuberculosis based on factors such as travel to Asia, smoking history, and X-ray results. Further details on the Asia network can be found at http://www.norsys.com/tutorials/netica/secA/tut_A1.htm.

The following is the diagram of the Asia network (courtesy of http://www.bnlearn.com/bnrepository/asia/asia.png):

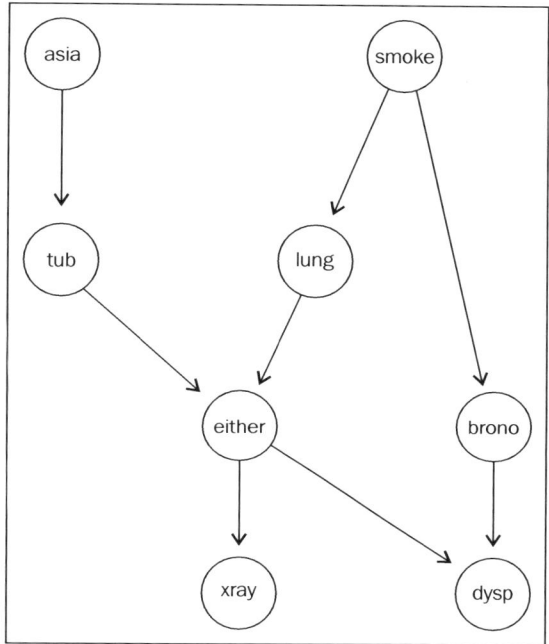

The goal of this code snippet is to compare two approaches to inference. The first approach is brute force, where we first list the entire joint distribution and then enquire about our probabilities. The second approach uses Variable Elimination, and we will study how it improves on the brute-force approach.

Suppose we wish to infer the probability that the patient has bronchitis $P(bronc = True)$; henceforth, this will be written as $P(bronc)$.

Let's first understand how we arrived at the value of $P(bronc)$ using the product rule, $P(smoke, bronc) = P(smoke) \times P(bronc | smoke)$. If we know $P(bronc | smoke)$, we can calculate $P(bronc = yes) = P(bronc = yes, smoke = yes) + P(bronc = yes, smoke = no)$. Also, $P(bronc = no)$ can be calculated in a similar fashion, and then the probabilities have to be normalized.

Exact Inference Using Graphical Models

We will load the network from a file where the network definition is stored as follows:

```
from libpgm.graphskeleton import GraphSkeleton
from libpgm.nodedata import NodeData
from libpgm.discretebayesiannetwork import DiscreteBayesianNetwork
from libpgm.tablecpdfactor import TableCPDFactor
import itertools
import pandas as pd
from libpgm.tablecpdfactorization import TableCPDFactorization

def loadbn(jsonpath):
    nd = NodeData()
    skel = GraphSkeleton()
    nd.load(jsonpath)
    skel.load(jsonpath)
    skel.toporder()

    bn = DiscreteBayesianNetwork(skel, nd)
    return bn

bn=loadbn("asia1.txt")
```

Our first attempt to compute marginal probabilities will use the joint distribution over all variables, and then sum out the variables we don't require. To list the joint distribution, we will multiply all the factors. The joint distribution computed from the product of factors is listed in the following code, and its complete specification has 255 entries:

```
#a method that prints the distribution as a table.
def printdist(jd,bn,normalize=False):
    x=[bn.Vdata[i]["vals"] for i in jd.scope]
    zipover=[i/sum(jd.vals) for i in jd.vals] if normalize else jd.vals
    #creates the cartesian product
    k=[a + [b] for a,b in zip([list(i) for i in itertools.product(*x[::-1])],zipover)]
    df=pd.DataFrame.from_records(k,columns=[i for i in reversed(jd.scope)]+['probability'])
    return df


#instantiate TableCPDs for all the nodes and multiply them. The result is in the factor that calls the methods.
jc=TableCPDFactor("asia",bn)
[jc.multiplyfactor(TableCPDFactor(i,bn)) for i in bn.V if i != "asia"]
```

```
df=printdist(jc,bn,normalize=True)
print "values in joint distribution ",len(jc.vals)
#print the first few values in the table
df.head()

values in joint distribution   256
```

The output of the preceding code is as follows:

Rows	dysp	xray	either	tub	lung	bronc	smoke	asia	probability
0	yes	yes	yes	yes	yes	yes	yes	yes	0.000013
1	yes	yes	yes	yes	yes	yes	yes	no	0.000262
2	yes	yes	yes	yes	yes	yes	no	yes	0.000001
3	yes	yes	yes	yes	yes	yes	no	no	0.000013
4	yes	yes	yes	yes	yes	no	yes	yes	0.000007

The preceding table lists the first five rows out of the 255 rows in the joint distribution.

Throughout this discussion, we will also overload the notation a bit. Since all the variables are binary, $P(bronc|smoke)$ means that the evidence variable smoke is true, unless otherwise mentioned, that is, $P(bronc|smoke)$ is the same as $P(bronc = True | smoke = True)$.

Marginalizing factors that are not relevant

From the joint distribution, we can get the desired marginal probabilities by performing the following operations. We are interested in data from the bronc column alone. So, we first collapse the other columns (and the data in them), in an operation called factor marginalization.

We shall use the Pandas data analysis library to manipulate the CPDs, which are akin to tables. After loading the joint distribution into a Pandas data frame, we will group only the columns we want and sum out the values in the probability column, as shown in the following code:

```
t2=df.groupby(['bronc','smoke'],as_index=False)
t3=t2['probability'].sum()
t3
```

The output of the preceding code is as follows:

Rows	bronc	smoke	probability
0	no	no	0.35
1	no	yes	0.20
2	yes	no	0.15
3	yes	yes	0.30

How does this operation happen? Let's take the 0th row in the preceding table (bronc == no, smoke == no) as an example and see how the value is obtained. The value of 0.35 is obtained by summing up all the values of the other columns. We will select rows of the table where all the values of bronc and smoke are no, as shown in the following code:

```
df.loc[(df["smoke"] == 'no') & (df["bronc"] == 'no'), :].head()
```

The output of the preceding code is as follows:

	dysp	xray	either	tub	lung	bronc	smoke	asia	probability
6	yes	yes	yes	yes	yes	no	no	yes	0.000001
7	yes	yes	yes	yes	yes	no	no	no	0.000024
14	yes	yes	yes	yes	no	no	no	yes	0.000119
15	yes	yes	yes	yes	no	no	no	no	0.002353
22	yes	yes	yes	no	yes	no	no	yes	0.000023

We will select all the rows from the preceding table and only choose the probability column. Then, we will sum up the values, as shown in the following code:

```
df.loc[(df["bronc"] == 'no') & (df["smoke"] == 'no'), "probability"].sum()
```

The output of the preceding code is as follows:

```
0.34999999999999998
```

We can see how the factor marginalization operation gives us a probability of 0.35 for the assignment (*bronc == no, smoke ==no*).

Factor reduction to filter evidence

Let's digress a bit to observe the case where the query had observed variables such as $P(bronc | smoke = yes)$. Then, we only need the first and the third rows from the previous table (with columns bronc, smoke, and probability). These rows correspond to $P(bronc = True | smoke = yes)$ and $P(bronc = False | smoke = yes)$.

This operation is called **factor reduction**, where the other rows are removed because they do not have the specific assignment for smoke(that is, the values are not yes), as shown in the following code:

```
t4=t3.loc[ (t3["smoke"] == 'yes'), :]
t4
```

The output of the preceding code is as follows:

Rows	bronc	smoke	probability
1	no	yes	0.2
3	yes	yes	0.3

This is almost the probability set that we require, except that the probabilities do not sum up to 1. We will, therefore, normalize by dividing each probability by the sum of all probabilities, as shown in the following code:

```
psum=t4['probability'].sum()
t4['probability']=t4['probability']/psum
t4
```

The output of the preceding code is as follows:

	bronc	smoke	probability
1	no	yes	0.4
3	yes	yes	0.6

Let's return to the original query that we had — *P(bronc)*. We've seen that the preceding table represents the conditional probability distribution of bronc when there is smoke. Now, we will simply sum out the value of smoke to get the value of *P(bronc)*, as shown in the following code:

```
t5=t3.groupby(['bronc'],as_index=False)
t5['probability'].sum()
```

The output of the preceding code is as follows:

	bronc	probability
0	no	0.55
1	yes	0.45

The preceding table gives the desired result of the inference query *P(bronc)*.

Shortcomings of the brute-force approach

What we have discussed previously is the brute-force method to arrive at the value of a probability query. This method is inefficient because of the following reasons:

- It does not use any of the conditional independencies that are present in the model. Let's say we want to know the probability of $P(A|B)$, and whether nodes X and Y are conditionally independent of A and B, then there is no point in calculating the joint distribution, which includes X and Y, and then summing out the values.

- We already know that eliciting the probability values in the joint distribution is not an easy task, nor is storing and manipulating the large joint distribution. For just eight binary variables in the alarm example, the joint distribution had 255 rows (or 2^8), and for larger networks, it becomes impossible to learn, store, and manipulate the joint distribution. Even after having the joint distribution, summing out the other values has a time complexity of $O(2^n)$.

Using the Variable Elimination approach

We shall now look at the Variable Elimination algorithm, which is an efficient method to calculate probabilities. The efficiency results from avoiding duplicate operations as well as avoiding calculation of probabilities that are conditionally independent. This algorithm can be used to calculate the marginal probabilities even if any evidence/observed variables exist.

We will use **Factors**, which are similar to the tables we have seen previously. The operations of **Factor product** (which is a Cartesian product between elements of two sets), **Factor Marginalization**, and **Factor Reductions** are the calculus by means of which we can manipulate **Factors**.

Each Factor has a scope. If we think of a Factor as a table, the variables in the scope are the table's column names. The eight CPDs defined in `asia.txt` are the initial factors. For example, the $\phi(tub, asia)$ factor has the variables `tub` and `asia` in its scope, and it corresponds to the $P(tub|asia)$ CPD. Similarly, the $\phi(lung, smoke)$ factor corresponds to the $\phi(lung, smoke)$ CPD. A CPD with multiple parents, such as $P(dysp|bronc, either)$, converts to the $\phi(dysp, bronc, either)$ factor, which has all the parents as well as the child nodes in the scope of the factor.

We list the factors in the `asia` network in the following list, along with the corresponding CPD they were derived from. The joint distribution involving all the variables will be the product of the factors in the list.

- $\phi(asia): P(asia)$
- $\phi(tub, asia): P(tub \mid asia)$
- $\phi(smoke): P(smoke)$
- $\phi(smoke, lung): P(lung \mid smoke)$
- $\phi(smoke, bronc): P(bronc \mid smoke)$
- $\phi(either, lung, tub): P(either \mid lung, tub)$
- $\phi(dysp, bronc, either): P(dysp \mid bronc, either)$
- $\phi(xray, either): P(xray \mid either)$

We will use the Variable Elimination algorithm to infer the conditional probability of $P(bronc \mid xray)$, which corresponds to a factor that has the same variables in its scope: $\phi(bronc, xray)$.

On scanning the preceding list of factors, we will see that there is no factor that has $bronc, xray$ in its scope. Therefore, to create $\phi(bronc, xray)$, we have to use the Factor product operation, where the variables in the scope of the resulting factor should appear in one of the factors being multiplied.

For example, the set of factors $\{\phi(smoke, lung), \phi(smoke, bronc)\}$ has three variables in its combined scope: $\{smoke, lung, bronc\}$. Therefore, the product of factors $\phi(smoke, lung), \phi(smoke, bronc)$ will give us a $\phi(smoke, lung, bronc)$ factor, where the probability values are derived by multiplying the row in the factor where the assignments match.

As the name suggests, in Variable Elimination, we eliminate variables one at a time. Each step consists of the following operations:

- Multiplying factors
- Marginalizing a variable (which is in the scope of all multiplied factors)
- Producing a new factor

Exact Inference Using Graphical Models

We will arrive at the $\phi(bronc, xray)$ factor in the following manner. Each row in the following table details one step of the algorithm, that is, the **Factor product**, the **Eliminated variable**, and the **New Factor created**, in pursuit of $\phi(bronc, xray)$.

Step No	Factor product	Eliminated variable	New Factor created
1	$\phi(asia) \times \phi(tub, asia)$	asia	$\phi1(tub)$
2	$\phi(smoke) \times \phi(smoke, lung) \times \phi(smoke, bronc)$	smoke	$\phi2(lung, bronc)$
3	$\phi(either, lung, tub) \times \phi1(tub),$	tub	$\phi3(either, lung)$
4	$\phi2(lung, bronc) \times \phi3(either, lung),$	lung	$\phi4(bronc, either).$
5	$\phi4(bronc, either) \times \phi(dysp, bronc, either) \times \phi(xray, either),$	either	$\phi5(dysp, bronc, xray)$
6	$\phi5(dysp, bronc, xray),$	dysp	$\phi6(xray, bronc)$

Out of the eight nodes in the graph, six are eliminated in each step, which leaves us with the factor we desire, $\phi6(xray, bronc)$.

We will use the `libpgm` library to walk through each step of the algorithm. The `libpgm` library gives us the `multiplyfactor` and `sumout` methods to create a new factor at each step. We have covered the first step in the following code:

```
asia=TableCPDFactor("asia",bn)
phi_1=TableCPDFactor("tub",bn)

phi_1.multiplyfactor(asia)
printdist(phi_1,bn)
```

The output of the preceding code is as follows:

Rows	asia	tub	probability
0	yes	yes	0.0005
1	yes	no	0.0095
2	no	yes	0.0099
3	no	no	0.9801

Since the starting factors are simply CPDs, when we create `TableCPDFactor("tub",bn)`, it is the factor that involves both `tub` and `asia`, which is calculated from the CPD for *tub|asia*. We will now eliminate `asia` by using the following code:

```
phi_1.sumout("asia")
printdist(phi_1,bn)
```

The output of the preceding code is as follows:

	tub	probability
0	yes	0.0104
1	no	0.9896

In the second step, we will multiply factors $\phi(smoke) \times \phi(smoke, lung) \times \phi(smoke, bronc)$, and eliminate smoke to produce $\phi2(lung, bronc)$, as shown in the following code:

```
phi_2=TableCPDFactor("smoke",bn)
[phi_2.multiplyfactor(TableCPDFactor(i,bn)) for i in ["lung","bronc"]]
phi_2.sumout("smoke")
printdist(phi_2,bn)
```

The output of the preceding code is as follows:

	bronc	lung	probability
0	yes	yes	0.0315
1	yes	no	0.4185
2	no	yes	0.0235
3	no	no	0.5265

In the third step, multiply factors $\phi(either, lung, tub) \times \phi1(tub)$, and eliminate tub to produce $\phi3(either, lung)$, as shown in the following code:

```
phi_3=TableCPDFactor("either",bn)
phi_3.multiplyfactor(phi_1)
phi_3.sumout("tub")
printdist(phi_3,bn)
```

The output of the preceding code is as follows:

Rows	lung	either	probability
0	yes	yes	1.0000
1	yes	no	0.0000
2	no	yes	0.0104
3	no	no	0.9896

In the fourth step, multiply factors $\phi2(lung, bronc) \times \phi3(either, lung)$, to eliminate lung and produce the $\phi4(bronc, either)$. factor, as shown in the following code $\phi4(bronc, either)$. We are not printing the CPD since we've seen what it looks like.

```
phi_4=phi_3
phi_4.multiplyfactor(phi_2)
phi_4.sumout("lung")
print "variables in scope ",phi_4.scope
```

The output of the preceding code is as follows:

`variables in scope   ['either', 'bronc']`

In the fifth step, multiply factors $\phi4(bronc, either) \times \phi(dysp, bronc, either) \times \phi(xray, either)$, to eliminate `either` and produce the $\phi5(dysp, bronc, xray)$ factor, as shown in the following code:

```
phi_5=TableCPDFactor("xray",bn)
phi_5.multiplyfactor(phi_4)
phi_5.multiplyfactor(TableCPDFactor("dysp",bn))
phi_5.sumout("either")
print "variables in scope ",phi_5.scope
```

The output of the preceding code is as follows:

`variables in scope   ['xray', 'bronc', 'dysp']`

In the final step, from the $\phi5(dysp, bronc, xray)$ factor, we will eliminate `dysp` to produce the $\phi6(xray, bronc)$ factor, as shown in the following code:

```
phi_6=phi_5
phi_6.sumout("dysp")
printdist(phi_6,bn)
```

The output of the preceding code is as follows:

Rows	bronc	xray	probability
0	yes	yes	0.055843
1	yes	no	0.394157
2	no	yes	0.054447
3	no	no	0.495553

The preceding factor has the `xray` and `bronc` variables in its scope, which we need, and since we need only a specific assignment of `xray=yes`, we can reduce the factor by the given evidence, as shown in the following code:

```
phi_6.reducefactor("xray",'yes')
printdist(phi_6,bn)
```

The output of the preceding code is as follows:

Rows	bronc	probability
0	yes	0.055843
1	no	0.054447

Since this is not a valid probability distribution, we have to normalize the probability by dividing it by the sum, as shown in the following code:

```
summ = sum(phi_6.vals)
phi_6.vals=[i/float(summ) for i in phi_6.vals]
printdist(phi_6,bn)
```

The output of the preceding code is as follows:

```
    bronc  probability
0   yes    0.506326
1   no     0.493674
```

The preceding code snippet details the steps involved in arriving at the required CPD.

When using the libpgm library, all the algorithmic steps are contained within the condprobve method; so, we just have to load the network and use that method, as shown in the following code:

```
bn = loadbn("asia1.txt")
evidence = {"xray":'yes'}
query = {"bronc":'yes'}
fn = TableCPDFactorization(bn)
result = fn.condprobve(query, evidence)
printdist(result,bn)
```

The output of the preceding code is as follows (observe that we get the same values obtained in the step by step procedure):

```
Rows  bronc  probability
0     yes    0.506326
1     no     0.493674
```

The Variable Elimination algorithm can be summed up as follows:

- The starting factors that are CPDs at each node
- Eliminate the nonquery variable Z from factors
- Multiply the remaining factors
- Repeat the same steps for all nonquery variables until only the query variables (and evidence/observed variables, if any) are left

The Variable Elimination algorithm works for both the Bayes as well as Markov networks. The algorithm completes once the set of nonquery variables in Z have been eliminated from the scope of all factors. While the variables in Z can be eliminated in any order (it results in the same final CPD), in the next section, we shall learn that optimized elimination ordering can help the algorithm terminate quickly.

Complexity of Variable Elimination

In the beginning of the previous section, we claimed that for inference queries, using the Variable Elimination algorithm is an improvement over querying the joint distribution. To better understand why variable inference is an improvement, we need to understand the algorithmic complexity of the algorithm.

We will start with m factors, and at each elimination step, we will generate one factor (by eliminating a nonquery variable). If we have n variables, we have, at the most, n rounds of elimination. The total number of factors generated, that is, m^*, will be less than $m + n$ (factors we start with, in addition to the eliminated n variables).

Let N stand for the size of the largest factor (the factor with the maximum number of variables in its scope).

Each step in the algorithm consists of deducing a Factor product and then summing out a variable, which is called a sum-product operation.

Therefore, the complexity is proportional to the number of sum-product operations. The product operations turn out to be less than $N \times m^*$, and the sum operations turn out to be $N \times n$. Therefore, the complexity is linear in terms of N and m^*, the size of the largest factor and the total number of factors generated.

Although the linear term appears, in truth, calculating the largest factor N requires exponential time. If a factor has four variables and all of them are binary valued, its complexity is $O(2^4)$. In the general case, v^k is the computational cost of computing a factor, if v is the maximum number of values a variable has in its scope (called its cardinality) and k is the number of variables.

Why does elimination ordering matter?

Although the Variable Elimination algorithm does not specify the order in which (non-query, non-evidence) the variables are eliminated, elimination ordering plays a role in the complexity. Let's look at the Markov network in the following diagram:

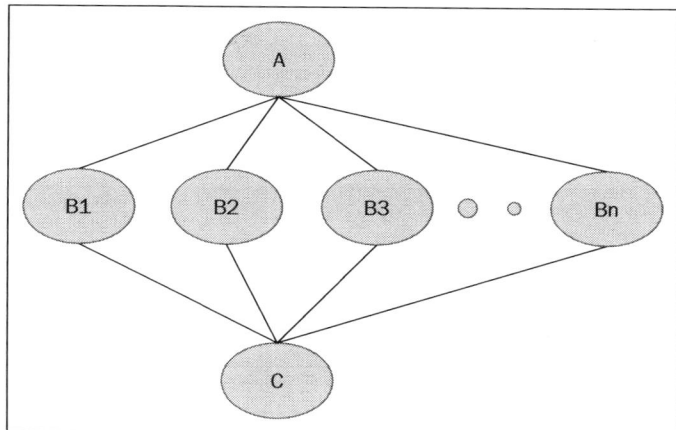

In the preceding network, suppose we choose to sum out or eliminate the variable **A**. We need to first have a product of factors $\{A, B_1, B_2..B_n\}$ and then sum out the variable. The factor that is created has a scope $\{A, B_1, B_2..B_n\}$, and it is exponential in n.

Instead, if we choose to sum out the variable B_1 first, the factor product results in a factor with scope $\{A, B_1, C\}$, which has only three variables. We've learned in the previous section that the complexity contains the term N (the size of the largest factor). Assuming that all the variables are binary, the difference in elimination orderings results in a complexity of 2^n for the first case and 2^3 for the second.

Since the complexity of the Variable Elimination algorithm is largely dependent on the size of the largest factor generated (which is exponential in scope), it is up to the elimination ordering to generate small intermediate factors to improve the runtime of the Variable Elimination algorithm. This example is taken from the Coursera PGM course, which can be accessed at https://www.coursera.org/course/pgm.

Graph perspective

While we were busy performing factor manipulation, the graph structure also changes with every factor multiplication and marginalization. We know that the factors and graph are just different representations of the same information; so, how does the elimination and creation of new factors affect the graph?

Since both directed and undirected graphs work the same way in the Variable Elimination algorithm, we can proceed with the analysis by assuming that the graph is undirected (even for a Bayes network).

Exact Inference Using Graphical Models

We'll look at an example of graph changes in the Asia network from the previous section. When we multiply to eliminate a variable, that is, the parent of the nodes in a scope, the resulting factor adds a link between the children in a process called moralization.

For example, in the second step of running the Variable Elimination algorithm for the Asia network, we will multiply factors $\phi(smoke) \times \phi(smoke, lung) \times \phi(smoke, bronc)$ and eliminate smoke to produce a new factor: $\phi 2(lung, bronc)$. This new factor represents the addition of a new link between the two nodes, as seen in the following diagram (the left-hand and right-hand sides indicate the variables before and after the second step is complete):

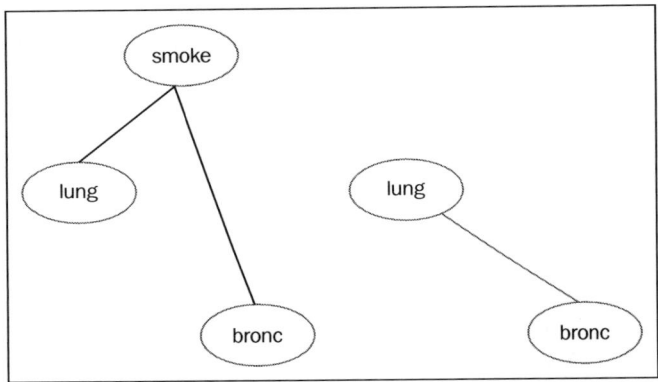

Why should the creation of a new factor require us to connect previously unconnected nodes? Since a factor encodes some independencies, the same independencies have to exist in the graph too. Therefore, as the process of Factor elimination and (new) Factor creation continues in the Variable Elimination algorithm, we add new edges to the graph to encode the same independencies. The Markov network created as a result of moralization is called the **Induced Markov network**.

For each factor that is generated in the Variable Elimination algorithm, the variables in the scope of the factor are connected by edges (that is, edges are added if they don't exist) called fill edges. The fully connected subgraph that corresponds to each factor is a minimal I-map for the distribution over the variables in that factor. You can recall that a graph G is a minimal I-map of a distribution P if the following conditions are satisfied:

- G is an I-map of P
- If $G' \subset G$ and G' is not an I-map of P

In other words, a minimal I-map is a set of independencies, and the removal of any edge from G causes it to cease being an I-map.

The edges added depend on the order of Variable Elimination (which determines the factors created as well).

Learning the induced width from the graph structure

Before we proceed to the discussion on the induced width, let's digress to remind ourselves about some terms used to describe the graph structure. A clique is a maximal, fully connected subgraph. Let's look at the following Markov network with four nodes:

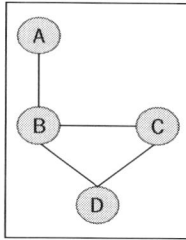

The nodes **B**, **C**, and **D** form a clique since they are all connected to each other. The clique is maximally connected since it cannot add any more nodes. The addition of **A** to the clique will fail the fully connected property.

Why does induced width matter?

The induced width is the number of nodes in the largest clique minus one. The minimal induced width is the least induced width obtained over all the VE orderings, which will be the lower bound on the best performance.

It turns out that every new factor created during a run of the VE algorithm is a clique in the Induced Markov network. Thus, the induced graph's cliques give us a quick approximation of the runtime of the VE algorithm. Even if we did find the best VE ordering (an NP-hard problem in itself), inference will still take exponential time, even with optimal ordering. Therefore, if we use optimal ordering and find that the clique in the induced graph has many (it's a relative number based on your hardware) variables in its scope, it may be time to ditch the exact inference methods in favor of approximate methods.

Finding VE orderings

Greedy algorithms are a fairly effective mechanism to find the best VE ordering. Several cost functions can be used, such as choosing the smallest factor first (a node with the least number of neighbors).

The tree algorithm

We will now look at another class of exact inference algorithms based on message passing.

Message passing is a general mechanism, and there exist many variations of message passing algorithms. We shall look at a short snippet of the clique tree-message passing algorithm (which is sometimes called the junction tree algorithm too). Other versions of the message passing algorithm are used in approximate inference as well.

We initiate the discussion by clarifying some of the terms used.

A cluster graph is an arrangement of a network where groups of variables are placed in the cluster. It is similar to a factor where each cluster has a set of variables in its scope.

The message passing algorithm is all about passing messages between clusters. As an analogy, consider the gossip going on at a party, where Shelly and Clair are in a conversation. If Shelly knows B, C, and D, and she is chatting with Clair who knows D, E, and F (note that the only person they know in common is D), they can share information (or pass messages) about their common friend D.

In the message passing algorithm, two clusters are connected by a **Separation Set (sepset)**, which contains variables common to both clusters. Using the preceding example, the two clusters $\{Shelly, B, C, D\}$ and $\{Clair, D, E, F\}$ are connected by the sepset $\{D\}$, which contains the only variable common to both clusters.

In the next section, we shall learn about the implementation details of the junction tree algorithm. We will first understand the four stages of the algorithm and then use code snippets to learn about it from an implementation perspective.

The four stages of the junction tree algorithm

In this section, we will discuss the four stages of the junction tree algorithm.

In the first stage, the Bayes network is converted into a secondary structure called a join tree (alternate names for this structure in the literature are junction tree, cluster tree, or a clique tree). The transformation from the Bayes network to junction tree proceeds as per the following steps:

- We will construct a moral graph by changing all the directed edges to undirected edges. All nodes that have V-structures that enter the said node have their parents connected with an edge. We have seen an example of this process (in the VE algorithm) called moralization, which is a possible reference to connect (apparently unmarried) parents that have a child (node).
- Then, we will selectively add edges to the moral graph to create a triangulated graph. A triangulated graph is an undirected graph where the maximum cycle length between the nodes is 3.
- From the triangulated graph, we will identify the subsets of nodes (called cliques).
- Starting with the cliques as clusters, we will arrange the clusters to form an undirected tree called the join tree, which satisfies the running intersection property. This property states that if a node appears in two cliques, it should also appear in all the nodes on the path that connect the two cliques.

In the second stage, the potentials at each cluster are initialized. The potentials are similar to a CPD or a table. They have a list of values against each assignment to a variable in their scope. Both clusters and sepsets contain a set of potentials. The term potential is used as opposed to probabilities because in Markov networks, unlike probabilities, the values of the potentials are not obliged to sum to 1.

This stage consists of message passing or belief propagation between neighboring clusters. Each message consists of a belief the cluster has about a particular variable.

Each message can be passed asynchronously, but it has to wait for information from other clusters before it collates that information and passes it to the next cluster. It can be useful to think of a tree-structured cluster graph, where the message passing happens in two stages: an upward pass stage and a downward pass stage. Only after a node receives messages from the leaf nodes, will it send the message to its parent (in the "upward pass"), and only after the node receives a message from its parents will it send a message to its children (in the "downward pass").

The message passing stage completes when each cluster sepset has consistent beliefs. Recall that a cluster connected to a sepset has common variables. For example, cluster C and sepset S have (x, y) and (y, z) variables in its scope. Then, the potential against y obtained from either the cluster or the sepset has the same value, which is why it is said that the cluster graph has consistent beliefs or that the cliques are calibrated.

Once the whole cluster graph has consistent beliefs, the fourth stage is marginalization, where we can query the marginal distribution for any variable in the graph.

We will now proceed to study an implementation of the junction tree algorithm.

Using the junction tree algorithm for inference

In the `JunctionTreeAlgorithm.ipynb` IPython Notebook, we shall use the **Bayesian Belief Network** (**BBN**) library to run exact inference using the junction tree algorithm. The library is available on Github (`https://github.com/eBay/bayesian-belief-networks`), and the documentation to install the library is mentioned on the Github page.

BBN has functionalities to load networks stored in the **Bayesian Interchange Format** (**bif**), which is developed by the Bayesian community to foster easier data sharing among different inference tools.

Once more, we shall use the `asia` network that we have seen earlier in this chapter.

After the mandatory imports, we parse the `.bif` format file with the `bif_parser` module, which returns a Bayes network object, as shown in the following code:

```
import bif_parser
import prettytable
import pydot
from IPython.core.display import Image
from bayesian.bbn import *

name = 'asia'

module_name = bif_parser.parse(name)
module = __import__(module_name)
bg = module.create_bbn()
```

We can view the Bayes network using the `graphviz` functionality offered by BBN (`graphviz` is a tool for graph visualization), as shown in the following code:

```
def show_graphgiz_image(graphviz_data):
    graph = pydot.graph_from_dot_data(graphviz_data)
    graph.write_png('temp.png')
    return 'temp.png'

sf=bg.get_graphviz_source()
Image(filename=show_graphgiz_image(sf))
```

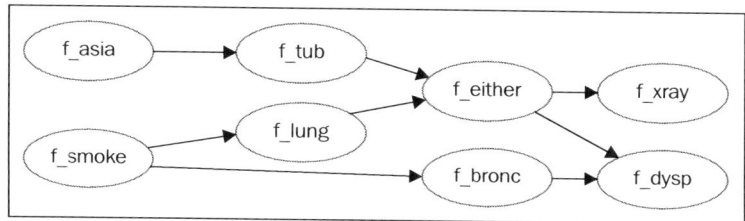

The preceding diagram shows us the network structure encoded in the `.bif` file. It is the same `asia` network that we saw earlier in this chapter.

Stage 1.1 – moralization

In the following snippet, we will view the moralization phase. Note that the V-structures, for example ,($f\_tub \rightarrow f\_either \leftarrow f\_lung$), have their parents moralized or joined with a new link.

```
gu=make_undirected_copy(bg)
m1=make_moralized_copy(gu,bg)
s2=m1.get_graphviz_source()
Image(filename=show_graphgiz_image(s2))
```

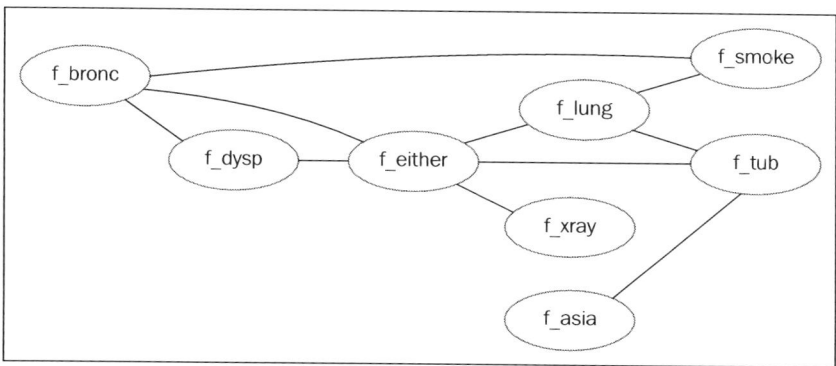

Stage 1.2 – triangulation

In the triangulation phase, the undirected graph is triangulated, which is the addition of edges between nodes if there is a cycle whose length is greater than 4. Note that in the preceding diagram, $f\_bronc, f\_either, f\_lung, f\_smoke$ forms a cycle with four nodes. In the following snippet, a link is added between f_either and f_smoke to triangulate it, which reduces the maximum length of the cycle to 3:

```
cliques, elimination_ordering = triangulate(m1, priority_func)
s2=m1.get_graphviz_source()
Image(filename=show_graphgiz_image(s2))
```

The output of the preceding code is as follows:

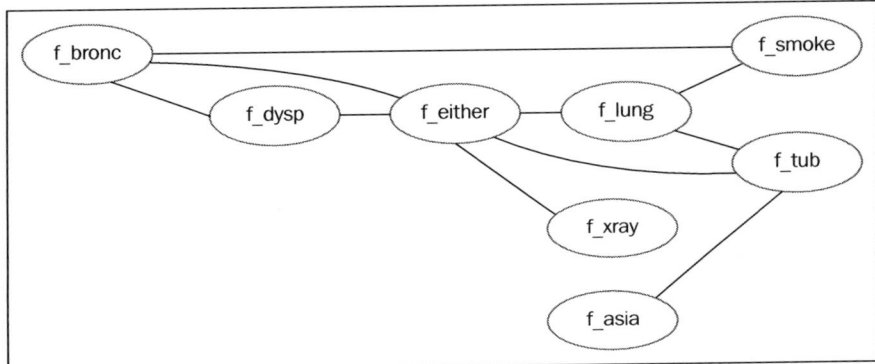

Stage 1.3 – building the join tree

Next, we will create the clique and the sepsets, which is done completely within the `build_join_tree` method. This method creates cliques according to the preceding graph and creates the sepsets which are the intersection points between every pair of cliques.

Note that the naming convention for the nodes in the generated graph is not exactly pretty. The `Clique_EITHERLUNGTUB` clique has the variables `either`, `lung`, and `tub` all smashed together.

```
jt=bg.build_join_tree()
sf=jt.get_graphviz_source()

Image(filename=show_graphgiz_image(sf))
```

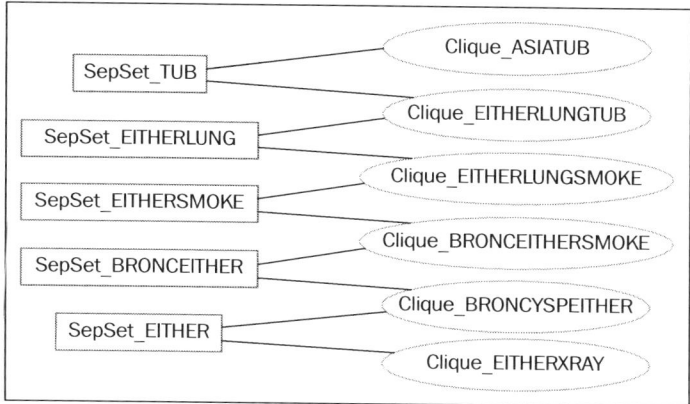

We can see from the variable names that the sepsets contain the intersection points of variables from the cliques that they connect with. For example, the variables in the cliques $\{Bronc, Either, Smoke\}$ and $\{Bronc, Dysp, Either\}$ are the variables in the $\{Bronc, Either\}$ sepset.

Stage 2 – initializing potentials

The next step is to create the initial clusters (which are usually the cliques) and initialize potentials, as shown in the following code:

```
assignments = jt.assign_clusters(bg)
jt.initialize_potentials(assignments,bg)
```

Stage 3 – message passing

Having built the structure required to run message passing, we proceed to the next stage. In this stage, there are two messages sent between each pair of cliques: one in a forward and another in a reverse pass.

The details of the message passing are contained within the `propagate()` method in the junction tree object. The sequence of messages in the network is shown in the following diagram:

```
Image(filename="../book/chapter6/images/9004OS_06_05.png")
```

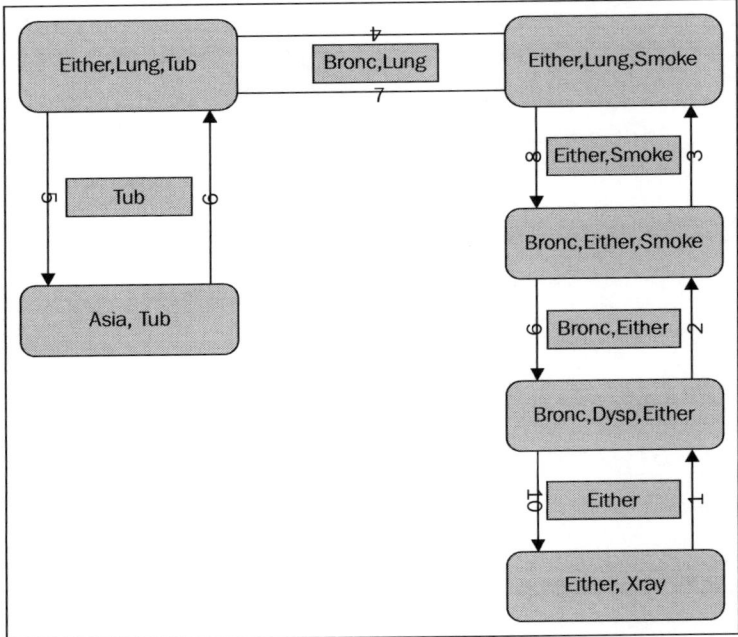

So what exactly happens when a message is passed? There are three actors in a message pass: the source cluster, the intervening sepset, and the destination cluster. Each of these has a set of potentials (very similar to a CPD along with the associated probabilities, except that it need not be a valid probability distribution).

For example, a message from $\phi_x(bronc, either, smoke)$ to $\phi_y(either, lung, smoke)$ would pass the $\phi_r(either, smoke)$ sepset, where the variables are in the scope of each cluster or sepset.

The message will modify the potentials at ϕr and ϕy, that is, the sepset potential and the destination cluster potential.

The first assignment to the sepset R are the potentials in the source with the variables not in the sepset marginalized out, as shown in the following formula:

$$\phi R = \sum_{X \setminus R} \phi x$$

The second assignment to the cluster Y is as follows:

$$\phi Y = \phi Y \frac{\phi R}{\phi_R^{old}}$$

Let's run the message passing bit using the `propagate()` method, as shown in the following code. This will run message passing between all the variables and will stop when the beliefs have converged.

```
jt.propagate()
```

Once all the message passing is done, we are left with a tree that has consistent beliefs in all its clusters.

On querying for a particular variable (for example, `bronc`), we just have to find a cluster (or a sepset) that has `bronc` in its scope and marginalize the other variables. The cluster printed here has `bronc`, `dysp`, and `either` variables in its scope. We printed all the potentials associated with this cluster. We can observe that each row lists the specific assignment to `bronc`, `dysp`, and `either`.

```
bronc_clust=[i for i in jt.clique_nodes for v in i.variable_names if v =='bronc']
bronc_clust[0].potential_tt
```

The output of the preceding code is as follows:

```
{(('bronc', 'no'), ('dysp', 'no'), ('either', 'no')): 0.4689219599,
 (('bronc', 'no'), ('dysp', 'no'), ('either', 'yes')): 0.008692680,
 (('bronc', 'no'), ('dysp', 'yes'), ('either', 'no')): 0.05210244,
 (('bronc', 'no'), ('dysp', 'yes'), ('either', 'yes')): 0.020282,
 (('bronc', 'yes'), ('dysp', 'no'), ('either', 'no')): 0.08282951999,
 (('bronc', 'yes'), ('dysp', 'no'), ('either', 'yes')): 0.003585240,
 (('bronc', 'yes'), ('dysp', 'yes'), ('either', 'no')): 0.3313180799,
 (('bronc', 'yes'), ('dysp', 'yes'), ('either', 'yes')): 0.032267160}
```

Let's try to find the marginal for `bronc` by marginalizing the `dysp` and `either` variables in the cluster by using the following code:

```
pot=bronc_clust[0].potential_tt

#a function to return the sum for a specific assignment, such as
'bronc,yes'
sum_assignments=lambda imap,tup:sum([v for k,v in imap.iteritems() for
i in k if i == tup])

#get the sum for bronc=yes and bronc=no
yes,no=[sum_assignments(pot,('bronc',i)) for i in ['yes','no']]

print 'bronc: yes ', yes/float(yes+no)," no ", no/float(yes+no)

bronc: yes   0.45   no   0.55
```

Since we claim that the junction tree is consistent, will other clusters that contain `bronc` return the same marginal values? Let's use the second cluster with `bronc` in its scope and marginalize on its potentials, as given in the following code:

```
pot2=bronc_clust[1].potential_tt
yes,no=[sum_assignments(pot2,('bronc',i)) for i in ['yes','no']]

print 'bronc: yes ', yes/float(yes+no)," no ", no/float(yes+no)
bronc: yes   0.45   no   0.55
```

We can see that we can obtain the same values of the marginal of `bronc` from two different clusters, indicating that the beliefs for all the variables are consistent across all clusters and sepsets.

> For an exhaustive introduction to the junction tree algorithm, refer to *Inference in Belief networks: A procedural guide*, by Huang and Darwiche at http://www.cs.iastate.edu/~honavar/bayes2.pdf.

In summary, both the algorithms presented in this chapter are similar in the principle that they use the same factor product and factor marginalization operations. Cliques in the clique tree are similar to factors used in Variable Elimination.

The junction tree algorithm has some advantages, such as the ability to answer several marginal queries in a single computation of a calibrated tree. Since the message passing is asynchronous, the algorithm can be parallelized and can return results quicker.

The disadvantage of the algorithm is that it is more expensive in terms of space. In Variable Elimination, the intermediate factors are not stored, but they are stored in the case of the junction tree.

Summary

We first explored the inference problem where we studied the types of inference. We then learned that inference is NP-hard and understood that, for large networks, exact inference is infeasible.

We then explored a couple of exact inference algorithms, such as Variable Elimination, and message passing, along with code samples that explain their fundamentals. We looked at the complexity of Variable Elimination and the ways to reduce its complexity.

In the next chapter, we shall look at the means of running approximate inference algorithms.

7
Approximate Inference Methods

In the previous chapter, we have learned that as the tree width of a graphical model increases, the exact inference becomes infeasible. The motivation to pursue approximate inference comes from real-world networks where the exact inference is intractable.

In this chapter, we will learn about the methods to calculate approximate inference. We will revisit message passing algorithms mentioned in the previous chapter and learn how they can also be used to calculate approximate inference when the network is not tree structured. We shall explore inference from the perspective of optimization and learn about sampling methods. We will also look at some code samples to understand how algorithms implement the approximate inference.

There are two general classes of approximate inference methods. In the first section, we explore inference as optimization, and in the second, we will explore particle-based inference methods.

The optimization perspective

In approximate inference, we seek to find or construct an approximation to the target distribution. Suppose we have the true target distribution P_ϕ, we seek to find a set of distributions Q that are easy to run the inference on, and then search among these easy distributions for the one that is "close" to the target distribution. The methods used seek to optimize the functions used to measure the distance or similarity between Q and P.

Casting the inference problem as an optimization allows us to draw on methods from the well-studied field of constrained optimization. One of the most used methods is to produce a set of equations that describe the optima of our objective function. In the context of graphical models, this method takes the form of a set of equations where each variable is defined in terms of other variables. It turns out that the equations that cast the problem as a type of a constrained optimization are equivalent to message passing over graphs.

In this section, we shall explore the belief propagation algorithm. In the earlier chapter, we ran belief propagation on tree-structured networks, whereas here we want to expand the discussion to networks that have other kinds of graph structures. This algorithm is called **Loopy Belief Propagation (LBP)** and is named thus because the cluster graphs can contain cycles and are sometimes called loopy.

Belief propagation in general graphs

Belief propagation is one of the message passing algorithms used for performing inference. Although it was first designed to run on tree-structured networks, it was discovered that it can also be used on general graphs that have loops or cycles.

There are a few differences in running the algorithm on a graph structure as opposed to a tree.

Tree-structured network	Graph-structured network
A node has to first receive messages from all its leaf nodes and only then send a message to its parents, and the whole process repeats in a downward direction.	While a node in a tree-structured network has the luxury of waiting for a message from its children before sending a message to its parent, in a network with loops, there is no straightforward procedure for a node to wait for messages before sending one out.
Only two messages are required to be passed between each node and its parent for convergence of beliefs to happen.	Message passing continues until the convergence is reached.
Message passing results in convergence of beliefs in the clusters and sepsets.	Convergence happens in most cases, but it is not guaranteed. Some networks might see oscillations and some might never converge.
The estimated marginals converge to the true marginals.	Even at convergence, the marginals might be incorrect, or the cluster beliefs need not necessarily be equal to the true marginals.

Creating a cluster graph to run LBP

The first task in running an LBP is to create a cluster graph when a set of factors is given. Each factor must be assigned to a cluster, but it is possible for one cluster to have multiple factors assigned to it. The conversion from a set of factors to a cluster graph is not unique. However, for a cluster graph to perform belief propagation, it must satisfy the following properties:

- **Running the intersection property**: If a variable X is present in two clusters, it should also be present in (all the clusters) the unique path that connects the two clusters.
- **Family preservation**: For every factor assigned to a cluster, the cluster's scope must include all the variables in the factor's scope.

Let's look at an example of a cluster graph creation.

We have the set of factors (along with the variables in the scope of each factor) shown in the following formula:

$$Z = \{F_1(A,B,C), F_2(C,D), F_3(E,F), F_4(B,D), F_5(E,D), F_6(D,F), F_7(D,H)\}$$

One possible cluster graph representation is shown in the following diagram. The variables in the sepsets are annotated on the edges that connect each cluster.

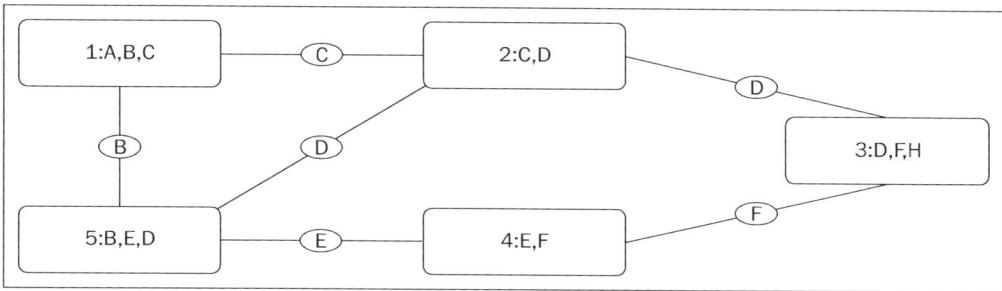

Note how the two properties mentioned previously are satisfied in the cluster graph.

- **Running the intersection**: The clusters **5**, **2**, and **3** contain the variable **D** in their scope. Running the intersection requires that, if **5** and **3** contain **D** in their scope, the cluster(s) between them should also contain **D** (cluster **2**).

Approximate Inference Methods

- **Family preservation**: The cluster-factor assignment is described in the following table (note that the cluster's scope includes all the variables in the scope of its assigned factors):

Clusters	Factors
1:A,B,C	$F_1(A,B,C)$
2:C,D	$F_2(C,D)$
3:D,F,H	$F_6(D,F), F_7(D,H)$
4:E,F	$F_3(E,F)$
5:B,E,D	$F_4(B,D), F_5(E,D)$

Message passing in LBP

Before any messages are passed, the initial beliefs at each cluster are simply the product of all the factors assigned to it.

Message passing proceeds in a similar fashion as we've seen in the previous chapter. First, all the messages are assigned a value 1. We shall denote M_{xy} as the message passed from the source cluster X to the destination cluster Y. We shall examine the M_{12} and M_{21} messages passed between the C1 and C2 clusters and other messages sent in that context in detail.

- M_{51}: These are the beliefs about the variable B sent from C5 to C1.
- M_{12}: These are the beliefs about the variable C sent from C1 to C2. This is done by performing the following steps:
    - Taking the existing beliefs at C1
    - Multiplying the incoming message M_{51}
    - Summing out variables A and B and calculating the message as follows:

    $$M_{12} = \sum_{a,b} F_1(A, B, C) M_{51}(B)$$

    - Sending M_{12} to C2
- We will fast forward to a few time periods later, during which the following messages were sent:
    - M_{52}: These are the beliefs about the variable D sent from C5 to C2
    - M_{32}: These are the beliefs about the variable D sent from C3 to C2

- We are now ready to send a return message M_{21} from C2 to C1. Recall that earlier, cluster **1** had sent its beliefs (about the common variable C) learned from its part of the network to cluster **2**, which now responds with its beliefs about the variable C. It creates the message in the following manner:
    - Taking the existing beliefs at C2
    - Multiplying the incoming messages M_{52} and M_{32}
    - Summing out variable D and calculating the message by using the following formula:

$$M_{21} = \sum_{d} F_2(C, D) M_{32}(D) M_{52}(D)$$

    - Sending M_{21} to C1

Note that when the message is returned from cluster **2** to **1**, it avoids sending the information that cluster **1** sent in the first place, else the beliefs that were sent from cluster **1** are simply echoed back and forth (double counting), and they get stronger in the process.

The message passing continues in the same fashion described previously and is stopped at convergence. The cluster graph can be assumed to have converged when the sepset beliefs changes across time steps are within a predecided tolerance value. Also, each pair of cluster beliefs agree with the sepset beliefs (for the edge that lies between the pair of clusters).

Steps in the LBP algorithm

We can summarize the steps in the LBP algorithm as follows:

- Assign factors to clusters
- Construct initial potentials (multiply all the factors in a cluster)
- Initialize beliefs at each cluster
- Repeat the message passing step: choose a cluster pair and pass a message between them
- Test whether the convergence has occurred or stopped after n repeats
- Summarize beliefs at each cluster by multiplying all the messages received with their initial beliefs as follows:

$$\hat{a}_i(C_i) = \Psi_i \prod_{k \in N_i} M_{k \to i}$$

Here, the belief in the ith cluster is the product of initial belief Ψ_i and the product of all messages $M_{k->i}$ from all *k* neighboring clusters.

Improving the convergence of LBP

The LBP algorithm is one of the algorithms in the general framework of message passing algorithms. Variants of LBP attempt to optimize the performance by tuning the following:

- The duration of message passing.
- **The timing of messages (synchronous/asynchronous)**: Asynchronous message passing has been shown to have faster convergence as compared to synchronous message passing. It must be understood that convergence is a local property. Some clusters/sepsets converge sooner than others. If we are interested in marginals from a given sepset or cluster, we need not wait for the whole cluster graph to converge.
- **Paths along which messages are sent**: Variants of BP such as TRWBP (tree weighted) by Wainwright and TRW-S (a sequential tree-weighted BP) by Kolmogorov try to find a set of minimum spanning trees within a cluster graph, and for each spanning tree, pass only messages on those trees. These have convergence guarantees in certain conditions, which are improvements in the original LBP, which does not provide any convergence guarantees.
- **Smoothing or damping of messages**: This prevents oscillations and increases the chances of convergence.

Applying LBP to segment an image

Let's look at applying LBP to perform image segmentation in the `LBP_image_segmentation.ipynb` IPython Notebook.

Image segmentation is the process of partitioning an image into multiple segments (called super pixels). The outcome of an image segmentation algorithm will be assigning a class label to every pixel in the image. Image segmentation is useful in several fields such as object detection (pedestrian detection), medical imaging (locating tumors), and several others.

In this notebook, we will use the OpenGM library (`https://github.com/opengm/opengm`) implementation of the loopy belief propagation to segment an image.

OpenGM is a C++ library with Python wrappers that has several implementations of inference algorithms. Please refer to the OpenGM website for installation instructions. For the Python wrapper, OpenGM requires installation of HDF5 (http://www.hdfgroup.org/HDF5/) libraries as well.

We will first load the image and convert it into a grayscale image by using the following code:

```
import opengm
from matplotlib import pyplot as plt
import numpy as np
import matplotlib.pyplot as plt
import matplotlib.cm as cm
import Image

fname = 'cow_image.jpg'
image = Image.open(fname).convert("L")
arr = np.asarray(image).astype(float)/255
plt.imshow(arr, cmap = cm.Greys_r)
plt.show()
```

The following is the original image that we attempted to segment. A successful segmentation algorithm should be able to differentiate between the pixels assigned to the cow and those assigned to the background.

The image is stored in a numpy array, whose dimensions are 183 x 275 pixels. Each pixel contains a value between 0 and 1, where 0 is for black and 1 for white.

We will digress a bit to understand the energy-based models that OpenGM uses.

Approximate Inference Methods

Understanding energy-based models

We have 183 x 275 pixels in the image, and each pixel can take one of the two labels. Assigning a label to a pixel is called labeling. We wish to choose the correct segmentation out of the total number of labelings in this image. Given the size of the image, the number of possible labelings are $(183 \times 275)^2$.

The probability of a labeling ω, given the observed image features f, is $P(\omega|f)$. We wish to find the optimal labeling $\hat{\omega}$, which is the MAP estimate, using the following formula:

$$\hat{\omega} = \mathrm{argmax}\ P(\omega|f)$$

The probability of a particular labeling is defined as follows:

$$P(\omega) = \frac{1}{Z}\exp(-U(\omega))$$

Here, $U(\omega)$ is the energy of the configuration ω.

In this discussion, we shall use the following kinds of potentials:

The first potential called the unary potential is a factor that has only one pixel in its scope. Each pixel gets its own unary potential.

The second potential is a pairwise potential, which is a factor that has neighboring pixels in its scope. The diagrams, which we will see later, will clarify these potentials.

Given that we are using unary and pairwise potentials, the sum of potentials in the whole image represents the energy $U(\omega)$ of an image, when a particular labeling ω is given, as shown in the following formula:

$$U(\omega) = \sum_{i \in C_1} V_{c1}(\omega_i) + \sum_{i,j \in C_2} V_{c2}(\omega_i, \omega_j)$$

Here, the first term and the second term at the right-hand side indicate the unary and pairwise potentials. C_1 and C_2 indicate factors that have 1 and 2 pixels in their scope, respectively.

Thus, an optimum labeling or configuration is the one that has the least energy given a particular assignment of labels to pixels. The goal of image segmentation is to find this optimum configuration.

For a detailed introduction on MRFs for image segmentation, please refer to `http://www.inf.u-szeged.hu/~kato/teaching/emm/multi-layer-mrf.pdf`.

Visualizing unary and pairwise factors on a 3 x 3 grid

Before you attempt image segmentation, let's try to understand the structure of the Markov network using OpenGM's model visualization.

In the following snippet, we will create a Markov network with nine nodes, arranged in a 3 x 3 grid.

The following diagram is the Markov network, where the random variables numbered from **0** to **8** are indicated in white unfilled circles, and unary and pairwise potentials in black squares:

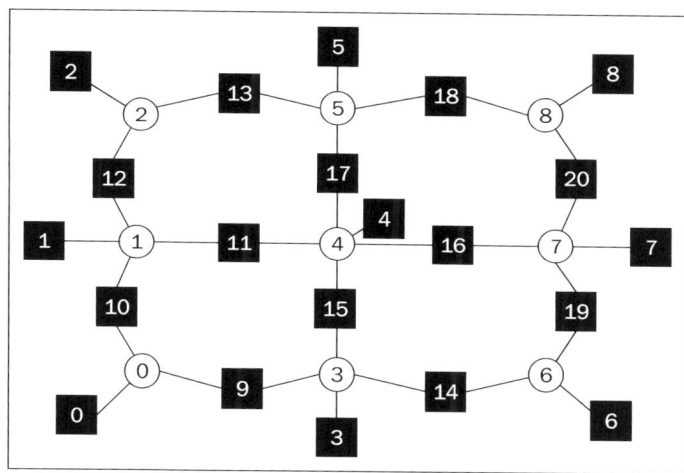

The `grid2d2Order` method creates the following sets of factors:

- The first set of factors includes unary potentials associated with each variable, and these are indicated in black squares numbered from 0 to 8, which are attached to each node. A unary factor's scope contains only the current node.

- The second set of factors includes pairwise potentials that connect adjacent nodes. These are also indicated in black squares numbered from 9 to 20. A pairwise factor's scope contains two adjacent nodes. For example, the factor **13** in the diagram can be represented by $\phi_{13}(2,5)$, which indicates that 2 and 5 are the nodes in its scope. This factor models the interaction between two neighboring nodes in a grid.

```
numLabels=2
shape=(3,3)
```

Approximate Inference Methods

```
unaries=numpy.random.rand(shape[0],shape[1],numLabels)
potts=opengm.PottsFunction([numLabels,numLabels],0.0,0.5)
gm=opengm.grid2d2Order(unaries=unaries,regularizer=potts)
opengm.visualizeGm( gm,plotFunctions=False,
                plotNonShared=True,relNodeSize=0.9)
```

To compute the energy of the entire network, we need to evaluate the energy at each factor. In OpenGM, this is done by associating a function with each factor. We have used a `potts` function in the preceding snippet, which takes a value of 0 if the input variables (in the scope of the factor) agree, and a value of 0.5 if they do not.

The network has `21` factors, and the node on the edge (0) has three factors associated with it, its unary potential (0), and its pairwise potentials (9, 10). Similarly, the node in the middle (4) will have four pairwise potentials (11, 15, 16, 17), in addition to the unary potential (4).

```
print "number of factors:",gm.numberOfFactors
print "number of factors of node 0: ",gm.numberOfFactorsOfVariable(0)
print "number of factors of node 4: ",gm.numberOfFactorsOfVariable(4)
```

The output of the preceding code is as follows:

number of factors: 21
number of factors of node 0:   3
number of factors of node 4:   5

Creating a model for image segmentation

We'll create a Markov network with unary and pairwise potentials in the same manner as we did for the previously discussed 3 x 3 network. Instead of a 3 x 3 grid, we'll now have a grid that has the *size = length x breadth* of the image in pixels.

```
shape=img.shape
dimx,dimy=shape[0],shape[1]
numVar=dimx*dimy
numLabels=2
beta=0.1

numberOfStates=numpy.ones(numVar,dtype=opengm.index_type)*numLabels
gm=opengm.graphicalModel(numberOfStates)

#add Unary factors, assign Potts function to the factors
for y in range(dimy):
    for x in range(dimx):
        f=numpy.ones(2,dtype=numpy.float32)
```

```
        f[0]=img[x,y]
        f[1]=1.0-img[x,y]
        fid=gm.addFunction(f)
        gm.addFactor(fid,(x*dimy+y,))


#Adding binary function and factors

#create the pairwise function (Potts function)
f=numpy.ones(pow(numLabels,2),dtype=numpy.float32).reshape(numLabels,n
umLabels)*beta
for l in range(numLabels):
    f[l,l]=0
fid=gm.addFunction(f)

#create pairwise factors for the whole grid, and
#assign the Potts function created above, to each new factor.
for y in range(dimy):
    for x in range(dimx):
        #add a factor between each pair of neighboring nodes.
        if(x+1<dimx):
            #add a factor between a node and its neighbor on the right
            gm.addFactor(fid,numpy.array([x*dimy+y,(x+1)*dimy+y],dtype=op
engm.index_type))
        if(y+1<dimy):
            #add a factor between a node and its neighbor above.
            gm.addFactor(fid,[x*dimy+y,x*dimy+(y+1)])
```

The preceding code snippet does the following:

- Creates a graphical model that has the image height x, image width x, and number of labels in its label space
- Creates unary factors, one for each pixel
- Assigns a `potts` function to each factor
- Creates pairwise factors, one factor for each pair of pixels that are adjacent on the *x* axis, and similarly for the *y* axis
    ◦ Assign a `potts` function to each pairwise factor

We are almost ready to start running inference on the Markov network. OpenGM allows us to create a visitor class that can observe the process of inference. In the `visit` method, which is called at intervals, we can observe the energy minimization in progress. We can also observe how the label assignments to each pixel improve as the overall energy of the Markov network is reduced.

We then create an instance of the `BeliefPropagation` class and run inference on it. The LBP algorithm will pass messages between pixels, and beliefs are computed at each node. When the callback method is invoked, we view the energy of the current configuration by using the following code:

```
imgplot=[]

class PyCallback(object):
    def appendLabelVector(self,labelVector):
        #save the labels at each iteration, to examine later.
        labelVector=labelVector.reshape(self.shape)
        imgplot.append([labelVector])
    def __init__(self,shape,numLabels):
        self.shape=shape
        self.numLabels=numLabels
        matplotlib.interactive(True)
    def checkEnergy(self,inference):
        gm=inference.gm()
        #the arg method returns the (class) labeling at each pixel.
        labelVector=inference.arg()
        #evaluate the energy of the graph given the current labeling.
        print "energy   ",gm.evaluate(labelVector)
        self.appendLabelVector(labelVector)
    def begin(self,inference):
        print "beginning of inference"
        self.checkEnergy(inference)
    def end(self,inference):
        print "end of inference"
    def visit(self,inference):
        self.checkEnergy(inference)

inf=opengm.inference.BeliefPropagation(gm,parameter=opengm.
InfParam(damping=0.05))
```

```
#parameter=opengm.InfParam(damping=0.1)
callback=PyCallback(shape,numLabels)
visitor=inf.pythonVisitor(callback,visitNth=1)

inf.infer(visitor)
```

The output of the preceding code is as follows:

```
beginning of inference
energy    21002.9691286
energy    16100.9689678
energy    16082.888577
energy    16069.1768137
energy    16051.5650505
energy    16032.2630915
<rows elided>
..


energy    15824.9003709
end of inference
```

We saved the labelings at each intermediate step, and we will now view the first six class label vectors to observe how the algorithm proceeds to segment the image. We can see that the cow's shape is easily identified from the labels assigned to each pixel using the following code:

```
fig = plt.figure(figsize=(16, 12))
for (counter, im) in enumerate(imgplot[0:6]):
    a=fig.add_subplot(3,2,counter+1)
    plt.imshow(im[0],cmap=cm.gray, interpolation="nearest")

plt.draw()
```

Approximate Inference Methods

The output of the preceding code is as follows:

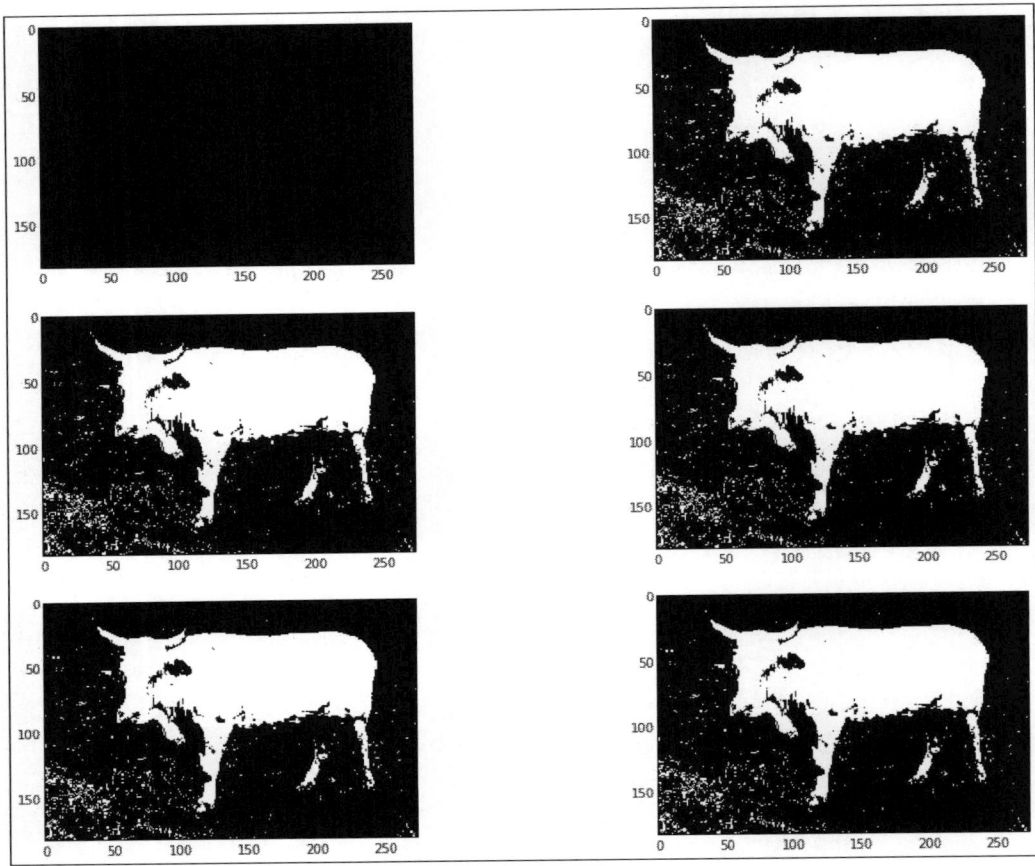

Finally, we will plot the final label assignment for each pixel, which is the **Maximum a posteriori** (**MAP**) assignment of class labels to pixels, along with the original image. This is the configuration that corresponds to the minimum energy.

```
fig = plt.figure(figsize=(16, 12))
a=fig.add_subplot(1,2,1)
plt.imshow(imgplot[-1][0],cmap=cm.gray, interpolation="nearest")
a=fig.add_subplot(1,2,2)
plt.imshow(img,cmap=cm.gray, interpolation="nearest")
plt.draw()
```

The following image is generated from the preceding code snippet:

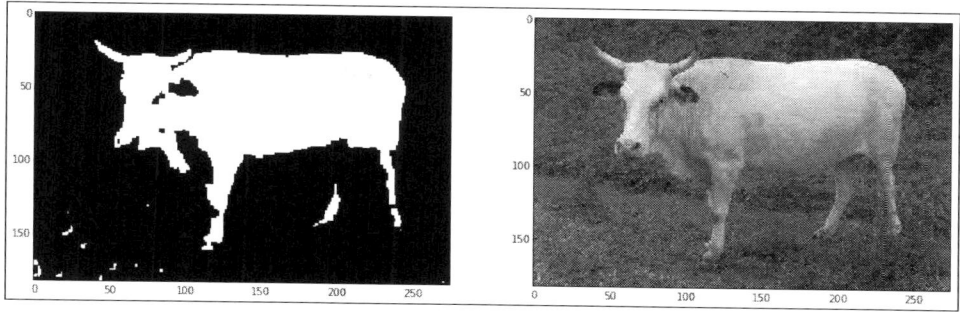

Applications of LBP

In the 90s, new methods of the high-performance code were discovered, which were close to the Shannon Limit (the theoretical maximum carrying capacity of a channel at which reliable communication is possible for a specific noise level). It turns out that the new code, called turbo code (http://en.wikipedia.org/wiki/Turbo_code), was implementing the LBP to achieve this improved performance, which resulted in a surge of interest in LBP and its variants in the field of approximate inference. As a result, LBP is now used in many fields that use the high-performance code such as mobile telephony standards, digital video broadcasting, mobile television, and deep space communications.

In summary, message passing is a widely used method for approximate inference. Inference is reasonably efficient for networks that are not densely connected. Although algorithms like LBP are not theoretically guaranteed to converge, its empirical performance is often quite good.

Sampling-based methods

We will now proceed to examine another approach to perform approximate inference.

In sampling-based methods, we use samples drawn from the distribution to estimate statistics from the overall distribution. The samples drawn are independent and identically distributed.

In the chapter on parameter estimation, we have drawn samples from the posterior distribution to estimate the probabilities of a CPD using methods such as maximum likelihood and Bayesian approaches.

In this section, we will learn to sample from a Bayesian network, which is slightly different from sampling a distribution.

Forward sampling

A sampling method that uses the topological ordering of a Bayes network is called forward sampling. A topological ordering in a Bayes network is an ordering of the nodes in the form $1, 2..n$ such that for every edge (i, j), we have $j > i$. If we traverse the graph in a topological order, all edges point forward. In other words, we sample the parents first and then descend to the leaves.

Let's look at the sampling procedure using the job interview network as an example:

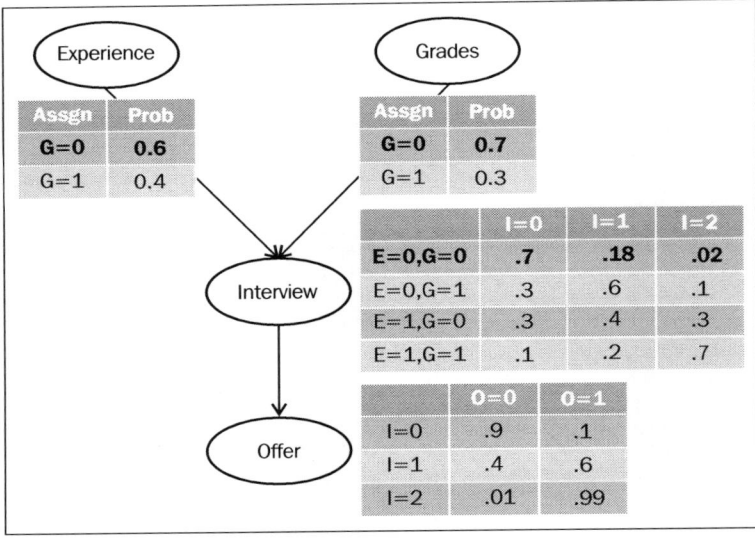

[136]

Note that the sampled entities are in bold text in the preceding diagram.

The following table shows an example of the sampling procedure. Each row of the table lists:

- The node we are sampling from
- The parent's sampled values (if any)
- The value sampled for the current node

Number	CPD	Evidence from parent's samples	The sampled value
1	Experience	-	$E = 0$
2	Grades	-	$G = 0$
3	Interview	Experience = 0, Grades = 0,	$I = 1 \mid E = 0, G = 0$
4	Offer	Interview = 1	$O = 0 \mid I = 1$

We thus arrive at a sample $\{Experience = 0, Grades = 0, Interview = 1\}$ $Offer = 0\}$ using one run of forward sampling.

To run an inference query such as $P(Offer = 1 \mid Interview = 1)$, we can use the samples to estimate the marginal probability using maximum likelihood. This can be achieved by taking the fraction of samples that satisfy the $Offer = 1, Interview = 1$ assignment, divided by the partition function.

The accept-reject sampling method

The accept-reject sampling method improves the forward sampling method to include evidence variables.

When we introduce evidence variables, we modify the sampling procedure in this manner: we first draw a sample, test whether it satisfies the assignment to the evidence variable, and reject it if it doesn't (and accept it if it does).

We know that to infer the marginal probability within a certain error tolerance, we'll have to draw a large number of samples. We can see that this method is wasteful, as it draws samples to reject a (possibly large) number of samples. Therefore to accumulate a large number of samples that satisfy the evidence is a time-consuming procedure.

Let's take an example of cancer testing. Suppose we wish to create a sample of patients who have breast cancer. The prevalence rate for breast cancer is about 125 per 100,000 patients (`http://seer.cancer.gov/statfacts/html/breast.html`). So, if we draw 100000 samples, we have to reject 99.875 percent of these samples since they do not conform to the observed evidence. If we were to have additional observed variables such as an age group between 20 and 30, Asian ancestry, male gender and so on, the chance of finding samples that satisfy these assignments becomes vanishingly small.

Thus, sampling for inference is a method that provides acceptable results in low dimensions. However, as the number of dimensions increases, or if the sampled assignments have a low probability, we'll need to turn to more efficient methods for inference.

The Markov Chain Monte Carlo sampling process

So far in our sampling methods, we have entertained the idea that each sample is independent. We can think of a dartboard as the surface we wish to sample, and each random sample is a hole left by a dart thrown at the dartboard.

We know that some of the sampling methods we have learned so far are quite inefficient, and therefore, designing efficient methods of sampling are critical to infer any statistics from distributions that are hard to sample from.

We can use an iterative sampling process called **Markov Chain Monte Carlo (MCMC)**. Using the dartboard analogy again, consider a grasshopper that is hopping on the dartboard. Every new spot the grasshopper jumps on can be considered a new sample. Samples drawn using such an iterative process are not independent and correlated with each other; however, we can encourage the grasshopper to proceed to the area where the samples of our interest lie.

We digress a bit to learn about a few properties of Markov chains before we learn about MCMC.

The Markov property

The Markov property states that if we have a sequence of states y_1 to y_k, then the transitioning to state $k+1$ depends solely on the state k. This is known as the first order Markov property.

The Markov chain

To understand a Markov chain, let's take the case of our friendly grasshopper.

The grasshopper has five stashes of food of varying sizes and constantly wanders around from one stash to another. Each transition (say from stash 1 to stash 2) has a probability associated with it, and there are also self-transitions (the grasshopper might start at stash 1, wander around, and come back to stash 1).

The following diagram depicts the transitions made by the grasshopper. Each edge has a non-negative transition probability associated with it.

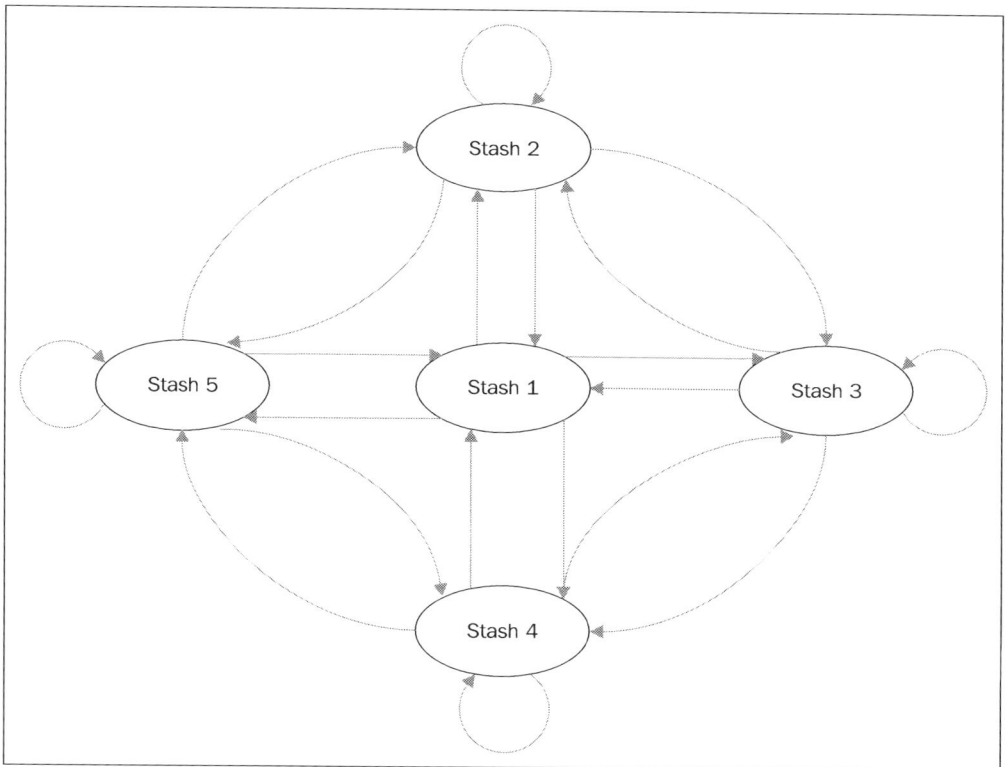

You may ask the question: what is the probability of finding the grasshopper at stash 1?

Reaching a steady state

It turns out that if we observe the grasshopper long enough, we'll arrive at what's called the stationary distribution. If we only observe the grasshopper for a short time, we can see that it spends 20 percent of the time at stash 1, 30 percent of the time at stash 2, and so on. However, if you observe the grasshopper long enough, regardless of which stash the grasshopper starts at, it will settle down to a stationary distribution, where the probability at time t is almost the same as at time t + 1 (the stationary distribution is also at the heart of Google's PageRank algorithm, where the grasshopper is replaced by a web surfer).

The grasshopper is an example of a Markov chain; it defines a transition model $T(x \to x')$ over all the states x. For all the states, the sum of their transition probabilities sum up to 1, $\sum_x T(x \to x')$ is equal to 1.

The transitions from states are defined in a transition matrix, and the *eigenvectors* of the transition matrix correspond to the unique stationary distribution over that set of states.

For a Markov chain to converge to a stationary distribution, it needs to adhere to the following set of properties:

- It is regular, that is, the probability of travel from any two pairs of states, say state x to y, in exactly k steps should be greater than 0
- The probability of transiting out of state x should be greater than 0, or there shouldn't be nodes that you can't transition out of
- All states should have self-transition.

Sampling using a Markov chain

What does building a Markov Chain give us? Using the grasshopper stash distribution analogy, we can think of our initial beliefs as the uninformative prior distribution (say, since the grasshopper has five stashes, the probability of finding the grasshopper at any stash is equal, that is, at 20 percent), and after the Markov chain achieves convergence (the grasshopper has wandered long enough), we can draw samples from the true posterior distribution.

A logical question at this point is just how long is "walking long enough". Unfortunately, there is no easy test to determine whether we have reached the stationary distribution (when we reach the stationary distribution, we can say that the chain has "mixed"). We can, however, use some statistical tests to find out if a chain hasn't mixed, and when those tests return negative answers, we can believe that the chain has indeed mixed.

To sample using a Markov chain, we first let the chain burn-in, which is the period where we believe the chain has not mixed yet, and once we are convinced that the mixing has occurred, we can collect samples and compute statistics.

To sum up, sampling using a Markov chain is easy to implement and has good theoretical properties, but in practice, the algorithm has many tunables. It is sometimes slow to converge, and determining whether a chain has mixed is a bit of an art.

Gibbs sampling

The Gibbs chain is a general-purpose sampler from the MCMC stable that can be used to draw samples from graphical models. This method is applicable when the conditional distribution of each variable is known or is easy to sample from. We will demonstrate one step of the sampling procedure in the next table, which describes the process of moving from one sample (x) to a new sample (x').

We start with a Gibbs distribution, that is, a product of factors, either from a Bayes network or a Markov network. The state space is the complete set of assignments to all random variables. The following is the example network that we intend to sample and contains three random variables that are connected as a V-structure:

$$X1 \rightarrow X2 \leftarrow X3$$

Steps in the Gibbs sampling procedure

The following are the steps involved in the Gibbs sampling procedure:

- Start with the current assignment to all variables
- For $j = 1$ to number of variables, sample each X_j variable, while the other variables hold their previous values

Approximate Inference Methods

In the following table, we follow each step of the sampling process for obtaining one Gibbs sample. We assume that the three random variables $X1, X2, X3$ are binary valued and the current assignment is $\{X1=0, X2=0, X3=0\}$. The cells in gray indicate that the value is fixed from the previous row, and the cell in white is being sampled.

Iteration	X1	X2	X3	
Starting values (x)	0	0	0	
Sample $X1 \mid X2=0, X3=0$	1	0	0	Flip a coin to select a value for $X1 \mid X2=0, X3=0$, we get 1
Sample $X2 \mid X1=1, X3=0$	1	0	0	Flip a coin to select a value for $X2 \mid X1=1, X3=0$, we get 0
Sample $X3 \mid X1=1, X3=0$	1	0	1	Flip a coin to select a value for $X3 \mid X1=1, X3=0$, we get 1
x'	1	0	1	This is the new Gibbs sample x'

The last row is the new state x', and the preceding table shows a single step of the Gibbs chain to generate the next state x'.

In summary, the Gibbs chain is the simplest Markov chain for graphical models. A Gibbs chain may not always be regular, that is, it may not arrive at a stationary distribution, but under certain conditions (such as positive factors), it is guaranteed to mix. It is one of the simplest Markov chains for PGMs but is slow to mix, especially when probabilities are peaked. It is only applicable when we can sample from a product of factors.

An example of Gibbs sampling

Let's look at a code snippet that compares random sampling and Gibbs sampling in the `Comparing Gibbs and Random Sampling` IPython Notebook.

In the following snippet, we'll first understand what it means to arrive at the stationary distribution for a discrete distribution and what methods we can use to get there faster.

We'll use the familiar job interview example to anchor the discussion.

The job interview network has five variables, and the joint distribution has 48 rows (2 x 2 x 3 x 2 x 2, the number of values each variable takes). We are interested in a marginal distribution over a subset of variables, and we have some observed evidence too.

We are interested in the marginal probability $P(\textit{Offer}, \textit{Grades}, \textit{Interview} \mid \textit{Admission}, \textit{Experience})$, where we have observed the values of the *Admission* and *Experience* random variables.

In the following snippet, we use exact inference (Variable Elimination) to determine the conditional probability, and then print the CPD for the same:

```
tcpd,bn,skel=getTableCPD()
query={'Offer':'0','Grades':'0','Interview':'0'}
evidence={'Admission':'0','Experience':'0'}
fac=tcpd.condprobve(query,evidence)
df=printdist(fac,bn)
df
```

The output of the preceding code is as follows:

	Offer	Interview	Grades	Probability
0	0	0	0	0.641455
1	0	0	1	0.029455
2	0	1	0	0.064145
3	0	1	1	0.026182
4	0	2	0	0.000178
5	0	2	1	0.000109
6	1	0	0	0.071273
7	1	0	1	0.003273
8	1	1	0	0.096218
9	1	1	1	0.039273
10	1	2	0	0.017640
11	1	2	1	0.010800

To get the desired distribution, that is, $P(\textit{Offer}, \textit{Grades}, \textit{Interview} \mid \textit{Admission} = 0, \textit{Experience} = 0)$, we first have to draw samples, and reject those that do not satisfy the evidence.

The libpgm library allows us to draw samples using random sampling and Gibbs sampling. In both cases, we can condition by the evidence ($\textit{Admission} = 0, \textit{Experience} = 0$).

In the following code, we draw 5000 samples using Gibbs and random sampling, and compare the marginal probabilities that are learned from the samples:

```
def estimate_distrib(skel,samples):
    learner=PGMLearner()
    #learn the parameters of the network from the samples, given skeleton
    #returns a new bayes net.
```

Approximate Inference Methods

```
            bayesnet=learner.discrete_mle_estimateparams(skel,samples)
            tablecpd=TableCPDFactorization(bayesnet)
            #run a conditional probability query for
            #P(Offer,Grades,Interview| Admission=0,Experience=0)
            fac=tablecpd.condprobve(query,evidence)
            #create a dataframe listing the marginals
            df2=printdist(fac,bayesnet)
            return df2

    #learn the marginals from gibbs samples
    def gibbs_marginals(num_samples=5000):
        tcpd,bn,skel=getTableCPD()
        samples=tcpd.gibbssample(evidence,num_samples)
        df2=estimate_distrib(skel,samples)
        return df2['probability']

    #learn the marginals from random samples
    def random_sample_marginals(num_samples=5000):
        tcpd,bn,skel=getTableCPD()
        samples=bn.randomsample(num_samples,evidence)
        df2=estimate_distrib(skel,samples)
        return df2['probability']

    df['prob from gibbs']=gibbs_marginals()
    df['prob from random samples']=random_sample_marginals()
    df
```

The output of the preceding code is as follows:

Offer	Interview	Grades	probability	P: Gibbs	P: random samples
0	0	0	0	0.641455	0.645444	0.078557
1	0	0	1	0.029455	0.025156	0.113443
2	0	1	0	0.064145	0.065997	0.058145
3	0	1	1	0.026182	0.026203	0.008655
4	0	2	0	0.000178	0.000000	0.013869
5	0	2	1	0.000109	0.000000	0.028531
6	1	0	0	0.071273	0.072956	0.048443
7	1	0	1	0.003273	0.002844	0.069957
8	1	1	0	0.096218	0.096203	0.504855
9	1	1	1	0.039273	0.038197	0.075145
10	1	2	0	0.017640	0.016400	0.000131
11	1	2	1	0.010800	0.010600	0.000269

The last three columns list the true probability (obtained from exact inference), the probability from Gibbs samples, and the probability from random samples. We can see that the probabilities from Gibbs samples are reasonably close to the true marginal values, and the random samples differ quite a bit from the true probability.

It is obvious that Gibbs sampling is a much more efficient sampling process than random sampling. Yet, for larger dimensions, Gibbs sampling will also struggle to obtain the marginal values that are close to the true marginal values.

Summary

In this chapter, we've learned the approach to solve problems that were deemed intractable by exact inference. The first method was inference as optimization, one of which was based on message passing.

The second method we studied was the particle-based inference (also called sampling). We learned how sampling struggles once the dimensions increase, and we also learned methods such as MCMC that allow us to use samples to get to the desired posterior distribution.

References

Chapter 1

- For the Bayes rule example on athletes using drugs, visit http://www.zweigmedia.com/RealWorld/tutorialsf3/frames6_6.html.
- *Sargur Srihari. Querying Joint Probability Distributions* (http://www.cedar.buffalo.edu/~srihari/CSE574/Chap8/Ch8-PGM-Directed/8.1.2-QueryingProbabilityDistributions.pdf).

Chapter 2

- For Libpgm, visit https://pypi.python.org/pypi/libpgm

Chapter 3

- The Coursera PGM course can be accessed at https://www.coursera.org/course/pgm

Chapter 4

- *Yang Zhou. Structure Learning of Probabilistic Graphical Models: A Comprehensive Survey* (http://arxiv.org/pdf/1111.6925.pdf).
- *Cassio P. de Campos, Zhi Zengat,* and *Qiang Ji. Structure Learning of Bayesian Networks using Constraints* (http://www.machinelearning.org/archive/icml2009/papers/246.pdf).

References

- BNFinder project location at http://bioputer.mimuw.edu.pl/software/bnf/.
- K. Sachs, O. Perez, D. Pe'er, D. Lauffenburger, and G. Nolan. "Causal Protein-Signaling Networks Derived from Multiparameter Single-Cell Data" (http://www.c2b2.columbia.edu/danapeerlab/html/pub/science2005.pdf).

Chapter 5

- PyMC documentation at http://pymc-devs.github.io/pymc/.
- *Probabilistic Programming & Bayesian Methods for Hackers* at http://camdavidsonpilon.github.io/Probabilistic-Programming-and-Bayesian-Methods-for-Hackers/.
- *Chapters on Parameter Estimation, Probabilistic Graphical Models*. Daphne Koller and Nir Friedman, The MIT Press.

Chapter 6

- *Inference in Belief Networks: A Procedural Guide*. Huang and Darwiche (the junction tree algorithm) at http://www.cs.iastate.edu/~honavar/bayes2.pdf.
- *DAGs, I-Maps, Factorization, d-Separation, Minimal I-Maps, Bayesian Networks*. Nir Friedman (http://classes.soe.ucsc.edu/cmps290c/Spring04/paps/nir2.pdf).
- Bayesian Belief networks project page at https://github.com/eBay/bayesian-belief-networks.

Chapter 7

- For information on OpenGM, visit https://github.com/opengm/opengm.
- *Loopy Belief Propagation for Approximate Inference: An Empirical Study*. Kevin P. Murphy, Yair Weiss, and Michael I. Jordan (http://www.cs.ubc.ca/~murphyk/Papers/loopy_uai99.pdf).

Other references

- *Machine Learning, A Probabilistic Perspective. Kevin Murphy.*
- *Probabilistic Graphical Models. Daphne Koller* and *Nir Friedman.*
- Coursera PGM course at https://www.coursera.org/course/pgm.
- *Bayesian Artificial Intelligence. Kevin B. Korb* and *Ann E. Nicholson* at http://www.csse.monash.edu.au/bai/book/about.php.

Index

A

accept-reject sampling method 137, 138
active trails, Markov network 45
Akaike information criterion (AIC) 62
alarm.csv file 57
approximate inference methods
   LBP algorithm 125
   optimization 121-122
   sampling-based methods 136
Asia network
   about 94
   URL 94

B

Bayesian Belief Network (BBN)
   about 112
   URL, for documentation 112
Bayesian information criterion. *See* BIC
Bayesian Interchange Format (BIF) 64, 112
Bayesian interpretation 11
Bayesian parameter estimation
   about 79, 80
   example 80-85
   example, for Bayes network 85-91
   for Bayes network 85
Bayesian score 63-68
Bayes network
   about 23
   chain rule 24
Bayes rule 9-11
belief propagation algorithm 122
BIC 62
BIC score 62
BNFinder tool 63

brute-force method
   about 100
   shortcomings 100

C

causal reasoning 25, 26
chain rule 24
clique 19, 109
clique tree-message passing algorithm. *See* junction tree algorithm
cluster graph
   about 110
   creating, for LBP 123
   example 123, 124
   family preservation 123
   intersection property 123
CompletedDirichlet variable 87
complexity, Variable Elimination algorithm
   eliminating 106, 107
conditional independence 15
conditional probability 9
conditional probability distribution (CPD) 23
Conditional Random Field. *See* CRF
constraint-based structure learning
   subset, finding of random variables 52, 53
   summary 60
   undirected edges, converting 54-60
   undirected graph, creating 54
convergence, LBP
   performance, optimizing 126
correlated features
   issues, in structured prediction 46
Coursera PGM course
   URL 107

CRF
  about 46
  example 47, 48
  representation 46, 47
cycle 20

D

data fragmentation
  about 77
  effecting, on parameter estimation 77, 78
Deterministic variable 81
Directed Acyclic Graph (DAG) 20
Dirichlet stochastic variable 87
discrete distribution 6
D-separation
  about 29, 31
  example 31, 32
  V-structure, blocking 33
  V-structure, unblocking 33

E

edge 19
eliminated variable 102
evidential reasoning 27

F

factorization
  about 34, 43, 44
  and independence 48
factor marginalization 97-100
factor product 100, 102
factor reduction
  about 98-100
  brute-force method, shortcomings 100
  calculating, Variable Elimination algorithm used 100-106
Factors
  manipulating 100
fill edges 108
flow of influence 44
forward sampling
  about 136, 137
  procedure 137
Frequentist interpretation 11

G

Gaussian distribution 7
Gibbs distribution 41, 42
Gibbs sampling
  about 141
  example 142-145
  steps 141, 142
graph structure
  about 107-109
  graph-structured network 122
  induced width 109
  tree-structured network 122
  VE ordering 110
graph terminology 19, 20
graphviz 113
grid2d2Order method 129

H

Hidden Markov Models (HMMs) 46

I

image segmentation
  about 126
  energy-based models 128
  Markov network, creating 129
  model, creating 130-134
  performing, LBP used 126, 127
  unary and pairwise factors, visualizing on 3 x 3 grid 129, 130
I-map 34, 35
independence
  about 14, 15, 20-23
  and factorization 48
  conditional independence 15
Independency map. See I-map
independent and identically distributed (i.i.d.) 70
independent parameters 20-23
Induced Markov network 43, 108
induced width 109
inference
  about 94
  complexity 93, 94
  real-world issues 94

installation, Python 20
inter-causal reasoning 27, 28
interpretations of probability
   about 11, 12
   Bayesian interpretation 11
   Frequentist interpretation 11

J

joint distribution 14
junction tree algorithm
   about 110
   join tree, building 114, 115
   message passing 115-118
   moralization 113
   potentials, initializing 115
   stages 111
   triangulation 114
   using, for inference 112, 113

L

LBP algorithm
   about 125
   applications 135
   applying, to image segmentation 126, 127
   convergence, improving 126
   steps 125
libpgm library
   about 102, 143
   URL, for installation 20
likelihood function 71
likelihood score 61, 62

M

MAP 16, 134
MAP queries 16, 17
marginal distribution 13
Markov chain
   about 139
   used, for sampling 140, 141
Markov Chain Monte Carlo (MCMC) 82
Markov chain Monte Carlo sampling process. *See* MCMC sampling process
Markov network
   about 39-41
   active trails 45

flow of influence 44
induced Markov network 43
pairwise Markov network 39-41
separation 45
Markov property 138
Maximum a posteriori. *See* MAP
maximum likelihood estimate. *See* MLE
MCMC sampling process
   about 138
   Markov chain 139
   Markov chain, used for sampling 140, 141
   Markov property 138
   steady state, reaching 140
message passing 110, 115-119, 124
message passing algorithm 110
Minimum description length (MDL) 62
MLE
   about 70
   used, for parameter estimation in Bayes network 74, 75
moralization, junction tree algorithm 113
Multinomial variable 87

N

Naive Bayes example 36, 37
nodes 19

O

OpenGM
   about 127
   URL 126
optimization, approximate inference
   about 122
   belief propagation algorithm 122
   cluster graph, creating for LBP 123
   constrained optimization 122
   message passing, in LBP 124, 125

P

pairwise Markov network 39-41
parameter estimation
   Bayesian parameter estimation 79, 80
   data fragmentation, effecting on 77, 78
   using MLE, for Bayes network 74, 75

parameter learning. *See* **also parameter estimation**
  about 69-71
  example 72, 73
  example, using MLE for Bayes network 75, 76
Partially Directed Acyclic Graph (PDAG) 20
Part of Speech tagging (POS tagging) 46
Perfect map. *See* **P-map**
performance-enhancing drugs (PEDs) 10
PGM
  references 147, 148
  structure learning 51, 52
P-map 34
potentials, junction tree algorithm
  initializing 115
probabilistic inference
  goals 8
probability
  about 5
  axioms 6
  conditional probability 9
probability distribution
  about 6
  discrete distributions 6
  Gaussian distribution 7
  uniform distribution 7
probability queries
  about 16
  evidence 16
  query 16
propagate() method 116
PyMC variables, types
  Deterministic 81
  Stochastic 81
Python
  installation 20

Q

queries 16
queries, types
  MAP queries 16, 17
  probability queries 16

R

random variables 13
reasoning, types
  causal reasoning 25, 26
  evidential reasoning 27
  inter-causal reasoning 27, 28

S

sampling
  performing, Markov chain used 140
sampling-based methods
  about 136
  accept-reject sampling method 137, 138
  forward sampling 136, 137
  Gibbs sampling 141
  Markov chain Monte Carlo sampling process 138
scipy
  URL, for installation 20
score-based learning
  about 60
  Bayesian score 63-68
  BIC score 62
  likelihood score 61, 62
  summary 68
separation, Markov network 45
Separation Set (sepset) 110
Stan
  about 94
  URL 94
Stochastic variable 81
structured prediction
  about 45, 46
  correlated features, issues 46
  CRF, example 47, 48
  CRF, representation 46, 47
structure learning
  about 51, 52
  constraint-based structure learning 52
  overview 52
  score-based learning 60
sufficient statistics 71
sum-product operation 106

T

**Term Frequency-Inverse Document
    Frequency (Tfidf)** 36
tree algorithm
  about 110
  junction tree algorithm 110
triangulation, junction tree algorithm 114

U

uniform distribution 7

V

Variable Elimination algorithm
  complexity 106
  complexity, eliminating 106, 107
  factor marginalization 97, 98
  factor reduction 98, 99
  graph structure 107-109
  used, for calculating factor
      reduction 100-106
  using 94-97
VE ordering
  finding 110
vertices. *See* **nodes**
V-structure
  about 30
  blocking 33
  unblocking 33

Thank you for buying
Building Probabilistic Graphical Models with Python

About Packt Publishing

Packt, pronounced 'packed', published its first book "*Mastering phpMyAdmin for Effective MySQL Management*" in April 2004 and subsequently continued to specialize in publishing highly focused books on specific technologies and solutions.

Our books and publications share the experiences of your fellow IT professionals in adapting and customizing today's systems, applications, and frameworks. Our solution based books give you the knowledge and power to customize the software and technologies you're using to get the job done. Packt books are more specific and less general than the IT books you have seen in the past. Our unique business model allows us to bring you more focused information, giving you more of what you need to know, and less of what you don't.

Packt is a modern, yet unique publishing company, which focuses on producing quality, cutting-edge books for communities of developers, administrators, and newbies alike. For more information, please visit our website: www.packtpub.com.

About Packt Open Source

In 2010, Packt launched two new brands, Packt Open Source and Packt Enterprise, in order to continue its focus on specialization. This book is part of the Packt Open Source brand, home to books published on software built around Open Source licenses, and offering information to anybody from advanced developers to budding web designers. The Open Source brand also runs Packt's Open Source Royalty Scheme, by which Packt gives a royalty to each Open Source project about whose software a book is sold.

Writing for Packt

We welcome all inquiries from people who are interested in authoring. Book proposals should be sent to author@packtpub.com. If your book idea is still at an early stage and you would like to discuss it first before writing a formal book proposal, contact us; one of our commissioning editors will get in touch with you.

We're not just looking for published authors; if you have strong technical skills but no writing experience, our experienced editors can help you develop a writing career, or simply get some additional reward for your expertise.

Mastering Python Regular Expressions

ISBN: 978-1-78328-315-6 Paperback: 110 pages

Leverage regular expressions in Python even for the most complex features

1. Explore the workings of Regular Expressions in Python.
2. Learn all about optimizing regular expressions using RegexBuddy.
3. Full of practical and step-by-step examples, tips for performance, and solutions for performance-related problems faced by users all over the world.

Parallel Programming with Python

ISBN: 978-1-78328-839-7 Paperback: 107 pages

Develop efficient parallel systems using the robust Python environment

1. Demonstrates the concepts of Python parallel programming.
2. Boosts your Python computing capabilities.
3. Contains easy-to-understand explanations and plenty of examples.

Please check **www.PacktPub.com** for information on our titles

Python 2.6 Graphics Cookbook

ISBN: 978-1-84951-384-5   Paperback: 260 pages

Over 100 great recipes for creating and animating graphics using Python

1. Create captivating graphics with ease and bring them to life using Python.
2. Apply effects to your graphics using powerful Python methods.
3. Develop vector as well as raster graphics and combine them to create wonders in the animation world.
4. Create interactive GUIs to make your creation of graphics simpler.

Machine Learning with R

ISBN: 978-1-78216-214-8   Paperback: 396 pages

Learn how to use R to apply powerful machine learning methods and gain an insight into real-world applications

1. Harness the power of R for statistical computing and data science.
2. Use R to apply common machine learning algorithms with real-world applications.
3. Prepare, examine, and visualize data for analysis.
4. Understand how to choose between machine learning models.

Please check www.PacktPub.com for information on our titles

Printed in Great Britain
by Amazon